Hearing From Heaven

Recognizing the Voice of God

Hearing From Heaven

Recognizing the Voice of God

BY

GLORIA COPELAND

Harrison House
Tulsa, Oklahoma

Hearing From Heaven:
Recognizing the Voice of God
Previously published as *Walk in the Spirit*
ISBN 1-57794-205-1   30-0556

10 09 08 07 06 05 04 03 02 01   10 9 8 7 6 5 4 3 2 1

Published by Harrison House, Inc.
P.O. Box 35035
Tulsa, Oklahoma 74153

Contents

Introduction

What I am about to share with you will change your life. It has changed mine and the lives of others who have put it into practice.

I am not the same person I was a year ago and I will not be the same a year from now. I am changing from glory to glory (2 Corinthians 3:18). Hallelujah!

Ken and I have made a commitment in our personal lives and in our ministry that we are going on with God, no matter what. We are laying aside every weight of this world and we are going forward. We are on fire with the fervent desire to do the will of God on the earth, and we're going to stay on fire!

I pray that God will stir your heart, and that after you have read this book, you will not be the same. Prepare to receive light from God's Word. Expect to change. Expect to grow. Open your heart to the Holy Spirit. Let Him do whatever He desires to do in your life. He wants you to succeed. Allow Him to work in your heart.

Lay aside whatever problems or worries that have burdened your mind and chained it to this world. Let the Holy Spirit reveal to you the world of the spirit. All the power and wisdom you need to overcome every obstacle and solve every problem is available right now in the spirit realm in God. All you have to do is tap into it—and I will show you how.

I love you,

Gloria

CHAPTER 1

Faithfulness

"For the Eternal's eyes dart here
and there over the whole world, as he
exerts his power on behalf of those
who are devoted to him."

2 Chronicles 16:9 MOFFAT

Faithfulness

The end of the age is coming quickly. This is not an hour of gloom—it is the hour of God's glory! The Body of Christ is writing the final pages of the history of the Church. We are about to witness the most magnificent display of God's power that the earth has ever seen. God told Moses, *"As truly as I live, all the earth shall be filled with the glory of the Lord"* (Numbers 14:21).

Every generation has had its role to play in God's ultimate plan. During the time of Moses, God manifested His power on behalf of the children of Israel in such spectacular ways that they commanded the respect of the Egyptians. When Moses led the Israelites out of bondage, they were truly regarded as God's people because of the unquestionable demonstration of His supernatural power.

I believe that our generation will experience that same high privilege. The day has come for God to raise up the Body of Christ—the glorious Church—without spot or wrinkle. This Church will command the respect of the world because it has the miraculous power of God in manifestation with signs and wonders! The Church will show forth the glory of God.

Moses was faithful, and God needed his obedience because Moses' job was to stretch out his hand in the earth and command the will of God to be done. God had to have someone who was loyal and would dare to act on His Word. When Moses stretched out his hand, God extended His hand and performed miracles and signs and wonders! God needs faithful, obedient people in this hour because He is going to once again show Himself strong in the earth.

God revealed Himself to the children of Israel as the covenant-keeping God—Jehovah. He performed whatever signs and wonders necessary to bring them out of the bondage of Egypt. God needed Moses. They worked together. God used Moses because Moses knew God's ways. *"He made known his ways unto Moses, his acts unto the children of Israel"* (Psalm 103:7). If Moses had not been faithful to know God's ways, the children of Israel would never have seen His acts. Moses' heart was loyal toward God, and he made himself available to God.

Today, the Spirit of God is dealing with us much in the same way as He dealt with Moses. We have experienced a move in the Body of Christ in which God has taught us His ways. We have learned to live according to the Word. We have been taught to walk by faith and not by sight, because God needs a body of people who have a solid foundation in His Word. He needs those who will not be blown to and fro by every wind of doctrine. He needs those who have made God's Word the final authority in their lives. Those who know how to depend on His Word will be the backbone of this move of the Spirit.

I believe that we are the generation which will usher in the coming of the Lord Jesus Christ. Before He comes, God will manifest Himself more intensely than He did during the time of Moses. He will pour out His Spirit on all flesh. Think of it—the Spirit of God revealing Himself to flesh!

Since Calvary, the only thing Satan has been able to use against the Church is the weakness of the flesh. He has had to depend on deception through the weakness of man's flesh in order to be effective in his work. His power in the spirit realm was broken when Jesus was quickened with eternal life and raised from the dead. Legally, Satan's hold over mankind was forever broken by the Lord Jesus Christ.

God has revealed Himself to our generation in the spirit. We have learned to hear God in our spirit and to know Him by His Word. For the most part, He has not revealed Himself in a way that we could see, hear or feel in the natural realm. We have had to walk by faith and not by sight.

Satan has reigned in the area of the flesh. This has been his only avenue. But now, God, in His mercy and love for man, is going to sweep into the realm of sight and sound by His Spirit with signs and wonders. In this final great harvest of souls, God is going to take over the flesh realm. Satan will have no place to call his own! But Jesus said that false prophets would also arise in the last days and show signs and wonders in order to deceive the very elect. This is why the Word of God must remain our foundation.

We Are the Workmanship of God

God is pouring out of His Spirit upon all flesh. We have been born again to live and operate in the spirit. We are God's workmanship, created in Christ Jesus, ordained of God unto good works (Ephesians 2:10). We have the Holy Spirit—God Himself— abiding on the inside of us! God has determined to reveal and manifest Himself in the earth in the Body of Christ.

The Body of Christ is made up of spiritual beings living in bodies of flesh, who are capable of manifesting the glory of God. Ephesians 4:24 says these beings are created after God in righteousness and true holiness. Even so, God has not been able to reveal Himself to the degree that He desires, because we have been dominated by the flesh.

By His Spirit, God is revealing how we can walk in the spirit and not be controlled by the flesh. As we fine-tune our lives to obey the promptings of the Holy Spirit, God will have available the vessels necessary to manifest Himself in the earth.

God is not looking for ability; He is looking for availability. He needs you and me to do the work that must be done. He must have people who are faithful. Good help has been hard for God to find.

I believe we are in the midst of the greatest outpouring of the Holy Spirit in the history of the human race. We have come to the end of this age by God's timetable. It is harvest time! God has a plan for this generation—to sweep the souls of this earth into the kingdom of God.

Supernatural power will be required to accomplish this great task, just as it was required to deliver the children of Israel! The Body of Christ will deliver the children of men from the power of darkness by the power of the Holy Spirit.

When God called Moses, He chose a man who would be obedient. Moses made mistakes, but God was patient with him and would not allow him to draw back. God needed him. Moses had what it took to accomplish the great feat of delivering Israel: He was faithful.

Today, we must be faithful. God needs us. His plan is to use us as He used Moses. He is requiring that we "sell out" to Him. He is looking to show Himself strong on behalf of those whose heart is perfect toward Him. *"For the eyes of the Lord run to and fro throughout the whole earth, to show himself strong in the behalf of them whose heart is perfect toward him"* (2 Chronicles 16:9). That word *perfect* in 2 Chronicles 16:9 does not mean that God is looking for those who have never made a mistake. It means "loyal, devoted, dedicated, consecrated, faithful." MOFFATT says, *"For the Eternal's eyes dart here and there over the whole world, as he exerts his power on behalf of those who are devoted to him."*

God is looking for those who are devoted, loyal, consecrated and dedicated to Him, to His plan and to His purpose. God wants your heart!

Deny Yourself, Not God

We have learned to practice faith. God wants us to learn to practice faithfulness. Jesus said, *"Whosoever will come after me, let him deny himself, and take up his cross, and follow me"* (Mark 8:34). To deny yourself is to disregard your flesh and your own desires, ambitions and interests.

In Galatians 5, we read that the spirit lusts against the flesh and the flesh against the spirit. This simply means that the desires of the outer man are in direct opposition to the desires of the inner man. To follow Him we must deny the desires of the flesh—or body—and we must follow after the desires of our inner man—our spirit—which has been reborn in the image of God.

This I say therefore, and testify in the Lord, that ye henceforth walk not as other Gentiles walk, in the vanity of their mind, Having the understanding darkened, being alienated from the life of God through the ignorance that is in them, because of the blindness of their heart: Who being past feeling have given themselves over unto lasciviousness, to work all uncleanness with greediness. But ye have not so learned Christ; If so be that ye have heard him, and have been taught by him, as the truth is in Jesus: That ye put off concerning the former conversation the old man, which is corrupt according to the deceitful lusts; And be renewed in the spirit of your mind; And that ye put on the new man, which after God is created in righteousness and true holiness.

(Ephesians 4:17-24)

We are to follow after the part of us that is made after God. This will lead to the highest and best life possible on earth.

Many have tried to walk in the integrity of God's Word without putting their hearts into it. They want the good things—health, prosperity, victory and blessings—without giving themselves to God and serving Him with their whole hearts.

Jesus said, *"This people draweth nigh unto me with their mouth, and honoureth me with their lips; but their heart is far from me"* (Matthew 15:8). You can confess the Word of God from now until Jesus comes, but if your heart is not right, it will not come to pass.

Set Your Priorities

God is requiring that we get our priorities right. The things of this world steal from us time and energy we should be giving to the things of the spirit. You can get so caught up in using your faith for the affairs of this world that your desire will be for the things of the world instead of for God.

Be cautious of the thorns of life. The Scripture says the cares of this world, the deceitfulness of

riches and the lusts of other things enter into the
heart and choke the Word until the Word cannot
produce (Mark 4:18-19). People who give their
thoughts and energy to gratifying the flesh will not
walk in the power of God.

I am not talking about sin. Obviously, we will
not consistently walk in the power of God with sin
in our lives. But I am talking about the attention
and affection of our hearts being given to this
natural, physical world instead of to God. We are
either walking after the natural world or after the
spiritual world.

Many have tried to have the best of both worlds.
You may have a little success that way, but you will
not experience the blessings and power of God to
the degree He desires for you. God requires more
of us because we have revelation knowledge of His
Word. *"For unto whomsoever much is given, of him
shall be much required"* (Luke 12:48).

We are a generation to whom much has been
given. God has not trained us in His Word so we
could consume it on our own lusts. He has revealed

His Word to us so we would walk in the spirit while we live in a natural, physical world. We have a job to do. He has taught us to use our faith to harvest souls.

We have to learn to walk in the spirit to fulfill God's plan for this hour.

A well-known preacher prophesied:

> *But as you walk with the Lord, as you prepare your heart, as you feed upon His Word, as you listen to what the Spirit of God says, your heart shall be prepared and your mind will be changed until you will flow in the supernatural as naturally as a bird will fly in the air. And you'll flow in the supernatural as naturally as a fish will swim in the water. And you'll flow in the supernatural as naturally as you will breathe the very air.*

We will not even be conscious of using our faith, because it will be so very natural and normal to walk in the spirit! But to do this we must let go of our allegiance to this natural world. It holds no security anyway. Jesus said, *"For whosoever will save his life shall lose it: but whosoever shall lose his life for my sake and the gospel's, the same shall save it"* (Mark 8:35). If we try to hold on to the natural things of this world instead of serving God with our whole hearts, we will miss out on the glorious things of the Spirit.

When Kenneth and I first heard about living by faith, we were in desperate circumstances. We didn't know any better than to be sick and in debt. It was easy to dedicate ourselves to the Word, because we had no other answer. We couldn't do anything else! We were broke! But as we honored God's Word, God honored His Word and prospered us. We came to a place where we were no longer desperate. We could do whatever we wanted to.

It takes a lot more faithfulness to be totally dedicated to God now that we are prosperous than it did when we were broke. Today we serve Him, not out of desperation, but because we love Him and are devoted to Him.

Just think about it. God has people in the earth who know how to use their faith. We know how to put the Word to work, and we are going to serve Him. Now God has something to work with…faithfulness!

The Faithful Servant Is Blessed

God needs us to reach to the ends of the earth with the gospel. We are the carriers of God's Word. We are the Word made flesh, just as Jesus was. If this world does not hear the good news about Jesus from the Church, it will never hear the good news at all.

We have the same opportunity Jesus had to do the will of the Father. He laid down His life in glory to come to the earth and condemn sin in the flesh, and to make a way for us to be born again. Now, as spirit beings with the life of God in us, we are capable of manifesting God's Spirit in this earth. We are to lay down our lives in the flesh, yield to the Spirit of God and obey Him. If that were not the plan, He would have raptured the Church a long time ago!

He came to set up His kingdom, and He did. We enter into that kingdom by grace through faith. We are messengers of God's grace, telling the world they can be born again by faith in Jesus Christ.

We have learned to walk by faith. Now we must be faithful with what we know and do whatever is necessary to harvest the souls on the earth. As we become more faithful to God than we are to ourselves, we will experience the power of God that we have sought. The Scripture says if we sow to the spirit, we will reap life and peace; but if we sow to the flesh, we will reap corruption and death (Romans 8:4-14; Galatians 6:7-8). Ours is a generation that will sow to the spirit.

God is calling us to be faithful and alert to spiritual things. Jesus frequently spoke about faithfulness. He said: *"Therefore be ye also ready: for in such an hour as ye think not the Son of man cometh. Who then is a faithful and wise servant, whom his lord hath made ruler over his household, to give them meat in due season?"* (Matthew 24:44-45).

I put my name by this verse in my Bible. "Gloria is a faithful and wise servant." I have made the decision to be faithful. You should do the same. No one can do it for you. Commit yourself to be a wise and faithful servant. Say from your heart, "God, You can count on me."

According to the parable in Matthew 24, *"Blessed is that servant, whom his lord when he cometh shall find so doing."* Doing what? Doing what he is told to do: Being faithful to his Lord. Jesus did not say any servant would be blessed. The slothful servant was not blessed. He was not enjoying the benefits of the faithful one. The faithful and wise servant was blessed of his lord.

In Matthew 25, Jesus told the parable about the wise and foolish virgins. He was making the same point: Those who were diligent and prepared were blessed.

Then Jesus continued to teach the disciples about faithfulness.

Don't Bury Your Talent

For the kingdom of heaven is as a man travelling into a far country, who called his own servants, and delivered unto them his goods. And unto one he gave five talents, to another two, and to another one; to every man according to his several ability; and straightway took his journey.

(Matthew 25:14-15)

The one who was given five talents made five more talents. The one who was given two talents gained two more. They were faithful with what was given them.

"But he that had received one went and digged in the earth, and hid his lord's money" (Matthew 25:18).

After a period of time, the master returned to reckon with his servants. They all reported what they had done with their talents. To the two who had invested theirs and increased them, he said, *"Well done, thou good and faithful servant: thou hast been faithful over a few things, I will make thee ruler over many things: enter thou into the joy of thy lord"* (verse 21).

Then, the last servant reported to him and said,

Lord, I knew thee that thou art an hard man, reaping where thou hast not sown, and gathering where thou hast not strawed: And I was afraid, and went and hid thy talent in the earth: lo, there thou hast that is thine. His lord answered and said unto him, Thou wicked and slothful servant, thou knewest that I reap where I sowed not, and gather where I have not strawed: Thou oughtest therefore to have put my money to the exchangers, and then at my coming I should have received mine own with usury [interest]. Take therefore the talent from him, and give it unto him which hath ten talents. For unto every one that hath shall be given, and he shall have abundance: but from him that hath not shall be taken away even that which he hath.

(Matthew 25:24-29)

When Jesus ascended into heaven, He gave to us His Name, His authority and His power. Then He gave us our assignments and sent the Holy Spirit to endue us with the power necessary to fulfill those assignments (Mark 16:15-20; Matthew 28:19-20; Acts 1:8, 2:1-4). He said to preach the gospel to every creature, to cast out devils and to lay hands on the sick. In Matthew 28, Jesus told the disciples to teach the converts to *"observe all things whatsoever I have commanded you."* The Body of Christ is to carry on exactly as Jesus did. We are to preach the gospel of the kingdom and heal the sick (Matthew 10:1-8).

You can look at Church history and see the talents the Master has given each generation. He has brought one revival after another, waiting for the Church to do what He commanded. Now we are entering into the revival of the glory of God and of the Spirit being manifested to all flesh. Jesus is giving this generation the responsibility of walking in the spirit so the glory of God will be revealed in us.

We have a foundation of the Word that other generations did not have. More is expected of us. Did you notice that the faithful servants entered into the joy of their lord? The higher life—the life that is lived in the spirit—is where the joy is! Only the faithful will find it.

It does not matter if you received five talents or two. God expects you to be faithful now. Grow right where you are and become faithful over what God has assigned you to do. Prove yourself to be faithful over little, and He will make you ruler over much (Matthew 25:21).

The wicked and slothful servant did not know his master very well. He did not trust his master, so he was afraid. His master was not a hard man who reaped where he hadn't sown. The slothful servant had no faith in his master because he did not know him.

You must become faithful and diligent to spend the time it takes to get to know God. Set apart time every day to fellowship with Him and get to know Him personally. When you know Him, you will trust Him. You will know that He rewards you for being faithful!

I don't want to be numbered among those who are unfaithful, because to whom much is given much is required. Those of us who have a solid foundation in the Word are like the ones with the five talents. We can't afford to hide our talents in the ground if we expect to be blessed. We have to use what God has given us for His glory. We have to be wise and faithful servants.

All that God is asking and urging us to do is to really live! We can't do anything for Him without His abundantly giving back to us. He is offering us the high life. He is asking us to live the quality of life that the whole world wishes they could find. They are seeking it in the things of this world but never finding it. This world has no peace.

God is urging believers to walk in this higher realm, where they can absolutely dominate the things of this earth! It is the blessing and joy of the Lord that we receive when we become faithful.

Did you know that when you are born again, you become a child of God, not a servant? You become a servant only if you want to. Tell God every day, "Lord, You can count on me. I love You, and I am here to serve You. I deny my own interests. I lay aside the pleasures of this life, and I make myself available to You today. What do You want me to do?"

When you come to that place spiritually, you will begin to walk in an area with God which you thought would be possible only after you got to heaven! God will take you to such heights that you will be amazed.

Are You Available?

How will we be able to walk in the spirit even though we are clothed with this flesh? We do this by spending more time pursuing the things of the spirit than we spend pursuing the things of the flesh. We will have to become dedicated to prayer and to fellowship with God. We will have to be dedicated to the Word of God and be willing to pull aside from this busy life around us to get alone with God so He can guide us, teach us and communicate with us.

If you spend time around people who have strong personalities, their lives will automatically affect your life. You will find yourself doing the things they do. Their mannerisms will rub off on you. You can't help it. It just happens. Well, if you spend enough time with God, He is going to rub off on you!

Moses said, "Who am I to talk to Pharaoh?"

And God told him, *Certainly I will be with you.* God was saying to Moses, *It doesn't matter who you are. It is Who I am that counts.* All Moses needed was to have God with him.

Your natural ability does not determine your usefulness. All you have to be is one who lives in the presence of God. He has the ability!

God does not look to us for ability; He looks for availability. Make yourself available to Him by praying in the spirit, worshiping and fellowshiping with Him. He will begin to manifest His character, His nature, His glory and His Spirit in you. And that is what He wants to do. He came to live inside you so He could radiate from the inside out! That's what happened with Jesus.

When Jesus was on the Mount of Transfiguration, the glory of God within Him radiated outward and He was transfigured. *"His face did shine as the sun, and his raiment was white as the light"* (Matthew 17:2). It will happen the same way in our day. God has never changed His ways. The glory of God will come from the inside of us—from the inner man—as we give ourselves totally to God and walk in the spirit. We were predestined to be conformed to the image of Jesus (Romans 8:29-30). God has reproduced Himself in the believer so He can show Himself to the world through the believer.

God desires that the earth be filled with His people who are full of His glory. Romans 8:18 says the suffering we experience in giving up the things of this world is nothing in comparison to the glory of God which will be revealed in us. This glory is not only going to fall on us from above, but it is also going to come out of us, for God is living inside us!

We are a group of people who are going to love God to the degree that we will choose to go into our prayer closets and intercede rather than to enjoy the pleasures of this world. It takes more dedication to do that than it does to preach. When you are in your prayer closet, nobody sees it but God.

What is the result? *"Be not deceived; God is not mocked: for whatsoever a man soweth, that shall he also reap. For he that soweth to his flesh shall of the flesh reap corruption; but he that soweth to the Spirit shall of the Spirit reap life everlasting"* (Galatians 6:7-8). When we sow to the spirit, we reap the high life— peace, prosperity, divine healing—all of the blessings of God. The blessings of God have always been offered to people who serve Him and love Him with their whole heart.

CHAPTER 2

Overcoming the Flesh

"If we live in the Spirit, let us also walk in the Spirit."

Galatians 5:25

Overcoming the Flesh

Have you noticed that sometimes you are aware of certain things before you even know what the Word says about them? That's because the Holy Spirit is in you, teaching you the truth (John 16:13). You hear things in your spirit and they float up into your mind: *You need to do this. You need to do that.* Sometimes you listen and other times you don't. You hear it and let it go. Then, later it comes back and you hear it all again. These are the promptings of your spirit by the Holy Spirit.

As we become more aware of the Spirit of God in our everyday affairs, we will be quicker to hear and obey those promptings. That is God's desire for the Body of Christ. The Holy Spirit is revealing the will of God to us in our spirit.

I have been prompted by the Holy Spirit to spend more time in prayer and in fellowship with God. I have talked with people from all over the world who are hearing the same thing. Believers everywhere who have determined to please God agree that He is calling the Body of Christ into a more personal communion with Him. He is calling us to spend time in prayer and fellowship in His presence daily.

I get excited when I hear others repeat the same things God has told me. That is how we are going to come into the unity of the faith. The Spirit of God speaks to believers all over the world. When you and I are in agreement with God, we will automatically be in agreement with each other.

A pastor in Detroit told me, "God said my mornings belong to Him." That is what God had revealed to me. I realized it was God's will for me to set aside at least an hour or two every day to spend time in His Word and in prayer. You may realize God has told you the same thing.

God will not chase us down and demand our attention. The Bible tells us that if we seek the Lord, we will find Him. James 4:8 says, *"Draw nigh to God, and he will draw nigh to you."* God sent Jesus to the cross so that fellowship with God would be restored. The price has now been paid. He has sent the Holy Spirit. And it is now up to us to take what He has done for us and in us and draw near to Him. We must seek Him.

It was through obeying the promptings of my spirit that I began to pray in the spirit at least one hour daily. Then God revealed it to me in His Word. I am convinced of the absolute necessity of my spending at least an hour a day in prayer.

In the beginning I didn't do very well. I would determine to get up early and pray for an hour, and then I would fall asleep while doing it! But when I failed, I didn't quit! I would just get up the next day, begin to pray, and stick with it until my mind and body would come into agreement with my spirit. The weakness of the flesh says, "Don't get up this morning to pray. Do it tomorrow." Procrastination is a real tool of the devil. We have to learn to be as persistent to succeed as Satan is to make us fail.

The Flesh Is Weak

All through the Scriptures we see that spiritual failure is due to the weakness of the flesh. The law was weak through the flesh (Romans 8:3). Thus, Israel failed God. Peter failed because of the weakness of his flesh.

In the Garden of Gethsemane, Jesus told His disciples, *"What, could ye not watch with me one hour? Watch and pray, that ye enter not into temptation: the spirit indeed is willing, but the flesh is weak"* (Matthew 26:40-41). I had always read that as if He was saying, "Pray that you don't enter into temptation." Jesus was telling them, however, that if they would pray, when temptation would come they would not enter into it. Luke's account is even clearer. *"Why sleep ye? rise and pray, lest ye enter into temptation"* (Luke 22:46).

Temptation will come. But if we will get our spirit to be ascendant over our flesh and our minds, we will not give in to it. We need to spend time communicating with God in order to keep our priorities right. This is the key to overcoming the weakness of the flesh.

Only hours after the incident in the Garden of Gethsemane, Peter was tempted and he denied the Lord. Had he prayed, he probably would not have given in to the temptation. Peter's heart wanted to follow the Lord. When Jesus warned Peter that he would deny Him, Peter said, "Oh, I would never deny You. I would die for You. I would go to prison for You." That was his heart speaking.

Jesus said, *"The spirit…is willing, but the flesh is weak."* Peter's heart was right, but the weakness of his flesh was his downfall. His flesh gave in to the temptation.

We want to please God. We want to serve Him with our whole heart. But we have to overcome the weakness of our flesh.

We are peculiar creatures, because when we enter into the salvation of God, we become new creatures in Christ Jesus. We become spiritual beings in natural bodies. Therefore, we must learn through the revelation of God by His Spirit how to function the way He intended for us to. The Holy Spirit will teach us how to walk in the spirit even while we live in a natural body.

God wants to use us to manifest His life and minister the gospel to the world. As long as we are in this flesh, we have the ability to minister to others who live in the flesh. Otherwise, we could just go home to be with the Lord. The Bible teaches us that to be absent from the body is to be present with the Lord, and that would be far better.

We have allowed our flesh to dominate us through a lack of knowledge and a lack of fellowship with God. The Lord is calling us to walk in the spirit and to allow Him to manifest Himself to this world by His Spirit. We are to habitually conduct ourselves in the sphere of the spirit.

But the Body of Christ as a whole has never done that, even though we have had the potential to ever since the Day of Pentecost. Some have come closer than others have, but the Church as a whole has never walked in the spirit as we are going to walk in our day.

In 1977, a well-known preacher prophesied that men on this earth will walk and talk and act like God. He said that religious people would mock them and say, "They think they're God." And the Spirit said, "No, they are not God; they are only children of God, agents of God, ambassadors of God who have been sent to do the works of God."

You and I are going to stand in that place in this hour, and the world will be astounded. They would never dream it could be possible for mere men to walk in so much power and authority. To do this we are going to have to put into practice what the Holy Spirit is teaching us. The more the Holy Spirit reveals the spiritual realm to us, the more we will conduct ourselves in it. *"If we live in the Spirit, let us also walk in the Spirit"* (Galatians 5:25).

The place to begin is to *"pray, lest ye enter into temptation."* The flesh will do whatever it is trained to do. If you give your attention to the sin in this world, your flesh will desire to practice sin and to follow after the spirit of the world. If you expose your flesh to the things of God, it will learn to behave and walk after the Spirit of God. Hebrews 5:14 in *The Amplified Bible* reveals that if we are mature, we have our senses trained to discern between good and evil by reason of practice.

If you are lazy, it is because you have practiced being lazy. If you are diligent, it is because you have practiced being diligent. Each one of us has things that hold us back from walking in the spirit. Otherwise, we would all look just like Jesus.

You don't get hooked the first time you smoke a cigarette. You have to practice it before it becomes a habit. Drinking alcohol is caused by the weakness of the flesh, even though a person may be born again and know better. Alcoholism is the result of practice. A person does not become addicted the first or second time he drinks. But if he practices, it will

become a habit. It is the same with drugs, adultery
or any other work of the flesh (Galatians 5:19-21).

Confronting Sin

As born-again believers, it is vital that we deal
with sin and the weakness of our flesh, according to
the Word of God. God has dealt with Kenneth
about sharing with the Body of Christ the
importance of removing sin from our lives. Why?
Because if ministers do not reprove the darkness,
people will feel free to continue in sin.

God is calling us to holiness. He is calling us to
live consecrated, dedicated lives before Him. We
must lay aside the weight and sin that so easily
beset us, and walk on with Him (Hebrews 12:1). It
is time to walk in the glory of God!

What are the sins that so easily beset us? The
world considers adultery and murder to be sins, but
they give little consideration to breaking the law of
love. Nevertheless, both social sin and failure to
walk in love will hinder you.

> Every one who commits (practices) sin is
> guilty of lawlessness; for [that is what] sin
> is, lawlessness (the breaking, violation of
> God's law by transgression or neglect—
> being unrestrained and unregulated by His
> commands and His will).
>
> (1 John 3:4, AMP)

Sin is outright rebellion against God's laws.
Envy, jealousy and strife are sins; and they shut the
door to the blessings of God and open the door to
the devil.

Sin destroys the sinner, and unforgiveness will
make you sick. Living in sin could cause you to die
young. Adultery is a killer. We have been in the
ministry long enough to see what it does to people.
We have seen children die because of their parents'
adultery. God didn't do it. Sin did it. You cannot
make sin work for you. *"The wages of sin is death"*
(Romans 6:23).

If you are living in sin, the way to overcome
your flesh is to cause it to obey the spirit. If you are
committing adultery, most likely your heart is

broken over it. You don't want to be driven by the lusts of the flesh. Thank God, you can get out of it quickly! You have an Advocate with the Father—Jesus Christ the righteous. Satan has to accept that. He can pull you into temptation if you allow him to, but he cannot keep you there. When you decide to change—when you confess that sin and turn from it and get things right with God—you are instantly forgiven (1 John 1:9).

Practice Godliness

The whole world around us is pushing sin. Television and radio are pushing immorality and adultery. The world's voice urges your flesh to follow after sin. The devil pulls at your flesh to get you to go the world's way. The world tries to convince you that you are being deprived of all the fun and glory of sin. If you expose yourself to the things of this world, your body is going to dominate you. But you do not have to conform to the world!

In Galatians 5:17 we find that the flesh lusts against the spirit and the spirit against the flesh. In the Greek, the word *lust* means "desire" or "strong desire." The body has a strong desire to rule the spirit. The inner man, or spirit, desires to control the body. Practicing the things of the spirit will cause you to overcome the desires of the flesh. It will cause your spirit to dominate the flesh. You can live without the torment of one being pulled against the other. Simply expose your flesh to the things of God instead of the things of this world. Practice godliness. Romans 8:6 says, *"to be spiritually minded is life and peace."*

As you retrain yourself, you will find that your unholy desires will subside. People become addicted to alcohol or tobacco by exposure. But the good news is that it works both ways. If you continually expose your flesh to God, in your mind and your body, you will enforce the things of God instead of the things of the devil. You will form new habits. You can come to the place where you habitually live after the things of God instead of the things of the world. Your desire will be for God and not sin. God's way will become your natural way of life.

The Lord has made some things very clear about Romans 6-8. These chapters all deal with the weakness of the flesh and the strength of the spirit.

Romans 6:11-14 says:

Likewise reckon ye also yourselves to be dead indeed unto sin, but alive unto God through Jesus Christ our Lord. Let not sin therefore reign in your mortal body, that ye should obey it in the lusts thereof. Neither yield ye your members as instruments of unrighteousness unto sin: but yield yourselves unto God, as those that are alive from the dead, and your members as instruments of righteousness unto God. For sin shall not have dominion over you: for ye are not under the law, but under grace.

When you are born again, you no longer have to be dominated by sin. You are re-created to live in the spiritual realm of God. You can walk in the spirit while you are here on this earth. *"Know ye not, that to whom ye yield yourselves servants to obey, his servants ye are to whom ye obey?"* (verse 16).

You walk in the spirit by yielding to and obeying the promptings of your spirit instructed by the Holy Spirit.

> **I speak after the manner of men because of the infirmity [or the weakness] of your flesh: for as ye have yielded your members servants to uncleanness and to iniquity unto iniquity [by training and practice]; even so now yield your members servants to righteousness unto holiness [by practice].**
>
> **(verse 19)**

Most people yield to the things around them because that is the easiest way to go. The spiritual walk is in direct opposition to the world around us. If we are going to let the world entertain us through their television programs, newspapers and magazines, then it will be very easy to walk after the flesh.

On the other hand, if we decide to spend time in God's Word and in prayer, it will become easy to follow after the spirit.

Overcoming Through Obedience

God has made a way for us to live successful, holy lives. If we will learn to walk in the spirit, we will win the war between the flesh and the spirit. We will still have opportunities to enter into temptation, but we will not yield to them.

> **For when ye were the servants of sin, ye were free from righteousness. What fruit had ye then in those things whereof ye are now ashamed? for the end of those things is death. But now being made free from sin, and become servants to God, ye have your fruit unto holiness, and the end everlasting life. For when we were in the flesh, the motions [or passions] of sins, which were by the law, did work in our members to bring forth fruit unto death. But now we are delivered from the law, that being dead wherein we were held; that we should serve in newness of spirit, and not in the oldness of the letter.**
> **(Romans 6:20-22, 7:5-6)**

Sin brings forth fruit unto death. If we serve God with the same diligence that we once served sin, the result will be holiness. We cannot serve God and sin at the same time.

As believers, we are not in the same condition as we were when we served sin. We have been made free from sin. We can now serve God. We serve Him by obeying the promptings of our spirit by the Holy Spirit inside us (Romans 7:6, AMP). We are no longer to serve the lust of the flesh and the ways of this natural world. We are born again. We are spirit, just as God is Spirit. So, we ought to walk after this new man inside and not after our bodies.

That ye put off concerning the former conversation the old man, which is corrupt according to the deceitful lusts; And be renewed in the spirit of your mind; And that ye put on the new man, which after God is created in righteousness and true holiness. Wherefore putting away lying, speak every man truth with his neighbour: for we are members one of another. Be ye angry, and sin not: let not the sun go down upon your wrath: Neither give place to the devil. Let him that stole steal no more: but rather let him labour,

working with his hands the thing which is good, that he may have to give to him that needeth. Let no corrupt communication proceed out of your mouth, but that which is good to the use of edifying, that it may minister grace unto the hearers. And grieve not the holy Spirit of God, whereby ye are sealed unto the day of redemption. Let all bitterness, and wrath, and anger, and clamour, and evil speaking, be put away from you, with all malice: And be ye kind one to another, tenderhearted, forgiving one another, even as God for Christ's sake hath forgiven you.

(Ephesians 4:22-32)

The Apostle Paul stated the dilemma of the believer in Romans 7:14-23. Paul made reference to a born-again man, a spirit in the likeness of God living in a natural body. His body wanted to live after the ways of the world; yet, his inward man delighted in God's ways. He said, "Oh, what a condition I am in! I want to do good, but how to perform it or walk in it I don't know!"

Doesn't that describe us to some degree? Before we were born again, we habitually followed the course of this world. This world is following Satan. He is the god of this world (2 Corinthians 4:4). The world is following him straight to death and hell.

When we are born again, our body does not change. It still wants to practice old habits.

The reason I didn't faithfully get up to pray every morning was not because I didn't want to. My heart wants to do anything that pleases God. It was my body that wanted to stay in bed and sleep. It has never wanted to get up at 5:30 in the morning and pray! But the more I did it, the easier it became. Here's why.

Paul said:

O wretched man that I am! who shall deliver me from the body of this death? I thank God through Jesus Christ our Lord. So then with the mind I myself serve the law of God; but with the flesh the law of sin. There is therefore now no condemnation to them which are in Christ Jesus, who walk

**not after the flesh, but after the Spirit. For
the law of the Spirit of life in Christ Jesus
hath made me free from the law of sin and
death. For what the law could not do, in that
it was weak through the flesh, God sending
his own Son in the likeness of sinful flesh,
and for sin, condemned sin in the flesh:
That the righteousness of the law might be
fulfilled in us, who walk not after the flesh,
but after the Spirit.**

(Romans 7:24-25, 8:1-4)

I recognized that I was a spiritual being in a
natural body. There is no judgment against me
when I walk in the spirit. When I am walking in the
spirit, I am a spiritual being in a natural body that
is trained to follow the Lord!

Re-created

When you walk after the promptings of the
spirit, you walk after the new man on the inside.
The law of the Spirit of life that comes out of that
new man will make you free from the law of sin

and death. Bondages will no longer be able to bind you. The law of the Spirit of life in Christ Jesus is more powerful than the law of sin and death. You could never have been born again if it were not so.

The moment you decided to make Jesus the Lord of your life—and acted on it—you were born again. All the devils in hell could not stop you. The law of the Spirit of life that is in Christ Jesus has made you free. You were re-created. You became a new creature in Christ Jesus (2 Corinthians 5:17). Old things passed away and, behold, all things became new! Now, walk after those new things. While you are still in this body and living in a world that is going in the opposite direction, you can look and act just like God by yielding to His Spirit. God gave you His Holy Spirit to make you holy as He is holy.

God is calling us to follow Him. He will reveal His glory in the earth through us. God wants us to walk in the same dominion and anointing that Jesus Himself experienced on this earth!

We would not dare say Jesus did not come in the flesh. He lived here in a physical body. The Bible says He was tempted in every way we are, yet He did not sin (Hebrews 2:16-18).

Jesus overcame sin in the flesh. He dominated His body through His spirit. He communicated with God. Jesus began His ministry on a 40-day fast. He took authority over His flesh from the very beginning. Jesus lived in submission to God by knowing God's Word and walking according to the promptings of His inner man, anointed by the Holy Spirit.

The Bible teaches us that Jesus' prayer life was absolutely amazing. He prayed for people all day long. Then He prayed all night, fellowshiping with the Father. The Scriptures say that He arose *"a great while before day,"* or before dawn, to pray. Jesus kept His flesh under submission by praying and spending time with the Father. That is exactly what He told His disciples to do. *"Pray, lest ye enter into temptation"* (Luke 22:46).

Why did Jesus come in the flesh? Because fallen man had been given over to sin. We were in a "sin body" with a "sin nature." There was no redemption for us. There was no escape from our predicament. Someone had to take our place and pay the price for our sin. Jesus paid that price and condemned sin in the flesh. He set you and me free from the power of sin.

We have been set free from sin in the flesh. Galatians 5:16 says that if we will walk after the spirit, we will not fulfill the lust of the flesh!

Religious men have placed a lot of rules on the believer and said, "You can't do this, and you can't do that." Laws are weak because of the weakness of the flesh. The Bible does not say, "Clean up your life and then walk in the spirit." It says that if you walk in the spirit, you will not fulfill the lust of the flesh.

Overcoming Through Dedication

The question arises: "If walking in the spirit is the key, how do I start?" Romans 8:5-13 is the answer.

For they that are after the flesh do mind the things of the flesh; but they that are after the Spirit the things of the Spirit. For to be carnally minded is death; but to be spiritually minded is life and peace. Because the carnal mind is enmity against God: for it is not subject to the law of God, neither indeed can be. So then they that are in the flesh cannot please God. But ye are not in the flesh, but in the Spirit, if so be that the Spirit of God dwell in you.

Now if any man have not the Spirit of Christ, he is none of his. And if Christ be in you, the body is dead because of sin; but the Spirit is life because of righteousness. But if the Spirit of him that raised up Jesus from the dead dwell in you, he that raised up Christ from the dead shall also quicken your mortal bodies by his Spirit that dwelleth in you. Therefore, brethren, we are debtors, not to the flesh, to live after the flesh. For if ye live after the flesh, ye shall die: but if ye through the Spirit do mortify the deeds of the body, ye shall live.

If you put your mind on the things of this world, you are going to walk after the flesh. You may not want to, but if you play around with the world long enough, you will go in that direction. If you continue in sin, you will become dominated by it. You will become a slave to whatever spirit you continually yield yourself to obey (Romans 6:16). It's your choice. Do you want to follow after your flesh, or do you want to mind the things of the spirit?

The reward of following after the spirit is life and peace. The whole world is seeking satisfaction, but they are seeking it in the things of this world. The people of the world have no peace. They are carnally minded. Peace and fulfillment will not be found in the things of the flesh.

A carnal mind is simply one that is not subject to the law of God. *The Amplified Bible* says that sin is *"lawlessness—being unrestrained and unregulated by His commands and His will"* (1 John 3:4). The carnally minded man thinks the way the world thinks. The spiritually minded man thinks God's thoughts. He keeps his mind on the things of the spirit. He conforms his thought life to the Word of God. There is no other way to enjoy life and peace than to be spiritually minded and subject to God (Romans 8:5-6).

As you yield your mind and your body to the ways of God, the life of God will come out of you and quicken your mortal body. Your spirit man will rise up and become dominant. The voice of your flesh will subside. You will overcome evil with good.

You will notice in the New Testament that the Apostle Paul wrote continually to the churches about mortifying the deeds of the body through the Spirit.

Romans 8:13-14 should be read together: *"For if ye live after the flesh, ye shall die: but if ye through the Spirit do mortify the deeds of the body, ye shall live. For as many as are led by the Spirit of God, they are the sons of God."* Led to do what? Led to mortify the deeds of the body! The Holy Spirit will prompt you or lead you to mortify the deeds of the body.

Listen to the Spirit

You cannot live in sin and expect the blessings of God. As you give your time and attention to spiritual things—the Word of God, prayer and fellowship with the Lord—you will hear the Holy Spirit. You will hear His promptings and He will show you how to walk in the spirit. But you have to dedicate yourself to God. You have to think about Him. You have to sow to the spirit. *"Be not deceived; God is not mocked: for whatsoever a man soweth, that shall he also reap. For he that soweth to his flesh shall of the flesh reap corruption; but he that soweth to the Spirit shall of the Spirit reap life everlasting"* (Galatians 6:7-8).

If you have been thinking, *I need to spend more time in prayer* or *Watching television all the time isn't good for me spiritually* or *I shouldn't talk about people the way I do,* then the promptings of your spirit are being led by the Holy Spirit. He is trying to pull you aside from the things of the world. He is leading you to give God control of your life.

Once you begin to respond and obey those promptings, you will notice that direction from the Lord gets stronger and easier to discern. The voice of your flesh will get quieter.

The Holy Spirit in you bears witness with your spirit that you are a child of God and a joint heir with Jesus Christ (Romans 8:16-17). This means that as a born-again believer, you have the life and nature of God in your spirit right now. Notice that this witness is in your spirit, not in your mind.

You have the ability to walk in the spirit in glorious liberty on this earth. You don't have to wait until you get to heaven to live free from evil. Jesus prayed that the Father not take us out of the world, but keep us from the evil in the world (John 17:15).

"Because the creature itself also shall be delivered from the bondage of corruption into the glorious liberty of the children of God" (Romans 8:21). That *"glorious liberty"* referred to is walking in the spirit! You must commit to that liberty. You cannot enter into it halfheartedly. You have to sell out to God and give Him your whole heart.

How to Overcome

For we know that the whole creation [every creature] groaneth and travaileth in pain together until now. And not only they, but ourselves also, which have the firstfruits of the Spirit, even we ourselves groan within ourselves, waiting for the adoption, to wit [to know], the redemption of our body. For we are saved by hope: but hope that is seen is not hope: for what a man seeth, why doth he yet hope for? But if we hope for that we see not, then do we with patience wait for it.

(Romans 8:22-25)

The day is coming when we are not going to have this flesh body. We will have a glorified body. We will take on immortality. We will be a spirit being in a spirit body! There will be no more war between our spirit and our flesh.

What do we do while we wait for the redemption of these bodies? We groan within ourselves, in the spirit, waiting for that day. Romans 8:26 tells us how to overcome the weakness of the flesh and to walk in the spirit, even while we live in this body. This revelation has changed my life and the lives of countless others.

> **So too the [Holy] Spirit comes to our aid and bears us up in our weakness; for we do not know what prayer to offer nor how to offer it worthily as we ought, but the Spirit Himself goes to meet our supplication and pleads in our behalf with unspeakable yearnings and groanings too deep for utterance.**
>
> **(Romans 8:26, AMP)**

How does He bear us up in our weakness? By enabling us to pray in the spirit. Praying in the spirit causes your spirit to dominate your flesh. Praying in the spirit applies spirit to flesh. When you pray in the spirit, you pray the perfect will of God. Your prayer knows no limitation. It is God the Holy Spirit speaking through your spirit to God the Father in the Name of God the Son. That is prayer that cannot be overthrown.

The *King James Version* translates the word *weakness* as "infirmities." Perhaps we have overlooked what was actually being said. The Greek word is singular and should have been translated "weakness."

Romans 6-8 talks about the weakness of the flesh and the strength of the spirit. He has not changed directions. He is talking about overcoming the weakness of the flesh.

The Holy Spirit is our Comforter, Counselor, Helper, Intercessor, Advocate, Strengthener and Standby (John 14:16, AMP). His ministry is to bear us up, to help us, to strengthen us. God knew that man was weak through his flesh. He said:

> **A new heart also will I give you, and a new spirit will I put within you: and I will take away the stony heart out of your flesh, and I will give you an heart of flesh. And I will put my spirit within you, and cause you to walk in my statutes, and ye shall keep my judgments, and do them.**
>
> **(Ezekiel 36:26-27)**

God does not expect you to overcome the weakness of the flesh, even by your new, born-again spirit. He gave you His Spirit to help you and strengthen you. Ephesians 3:16 says we are "strengthened with might by His Spirit in the inner man."

CHAPTER 3

The Holy Spirit Is Our Helper

"And in like manner also the Spirit lends us a helping hand with reference to our weakness, for the particular thing that we should pray for according to what is necessary in the nature of the case, we do not know with an absolute knowledge."

Romans 8:26, WUEST

CHAPTER 3

The Holy Spirit Is Our Helper

The Holy Spirit will strengthen you with might in your inner man to overcome the weakness of living in a natural body. *"But if the Spirit of him that raised up Jesus from the dead dwell in you, he that raised up Christ from the dead shall also quicken your mortal bodies by his Spirit that dwelleth in you"* (Romans 8:11).

The Holy Spirit does not do the strengthening by Himself. He comes to our aid. He is our Helper. When we pray in other tongues, the Spirit of God bears us up in the weakness of our flesh—the part of us that is earthy and natural—and brings us God's answer to the situation or problem.

Through the operation of the Holy Spirit within us, we are no longer held in bondage to the natural world. Our part is to give Him place and then yield the control of our lives to Him. This allows the supernatural power of God to flow in our behalf to bring to pass the will of God. When we give place to the Holy Spirit and obey Him, we are allowing God to be God in our lives.

The Bible says, *"He that speaketh in an unknown tongue edifieth himself"* (1 Corinthians 14:4). The phrase *edifieth himself* means "builds up himself." First Corinthians 14:14 says, *"For if I pray in an unknown tongue, my spirit prayeth."* We know that praying in the spirit is praying in other tongues. When we pray in other tongues, we allow the Holy Spirit to express His will through us. After the new birth, I think it is most important to give the Holy Spirit control over your life. Jude tells us that we— the beloved—are to build ourselves up on our most holy faith by praying in the Holy Ghost.

Whatever weakness of the flesh you have, praying in the spirit—in other tongues—will overcome that weakness and give you victory. If you will spend time praying in the spirit every day, you will find that earth's bondages can no longer restrain you. The law of the Spirit of life in Christ Jesus makes you free from the law of sin and death. The Holy Spirit Himself is enforcing your deliverance.

"For if I pray in an unknown tongue, my spirit prayeth, but my understanding is unfruitful" (1 Corinthians 14:14). Praying in other tongues is the groaning too deep to utter in our known language. We cannot articulate in our known language those things that are too deep for our understanding. When we pray in the spirit—in tongues—we are not praying according to our understanding, or our limited knowledge, but according to the unlimited wisdom and knowledge of God. We can pray beyond our knowledge. Thank God for praying in other tongues. It will overcome our lack of knowledge and spiritual insight.

If we had been taught after conversion to give place to the Holy Ghost by praying in other tongues every day, and to expect and obey the leading of the Holy Spirit, our Christian lives would be far different. Praying in the Holy Spirit and

obeying the promptings of our spirit would have
kept us under the control of the Spirit while we
renewed our minds with the written Word of God.

The believers Paul was teaching in the book of
Romans did not have the Word of God written in
a book. They had a letter from Paul. The complete,
written Word was not offered to them as it is to
us. But they could go on to perfection or spiritual
maturity by the operation of the Holy Spirit. Even
though we have the written Word as our textbook,
we must not fail to follow the Holy Spirit. In both
the Old and New Testaments, God has always
been willing to deal with His people, not only by
written statutes and ordinances, but also by His
voice. He admonished Israel to keep His Word
and obey His voice and He would be God in their
lives (Exodus 19:5; Jeremiah 7:23). When they
came before the walls of Jericho, it was His voice
speaking to them that gave them victory instead
of defeat.

There is another side to this. If Israel had not
been keeping the written statutes and ordinances,
they would not have heard the voice of God that

brought them deliverance. We must learn to follow both the written Word and the moment-by-moment direction of the Holy Spirit.

Praying in the spirit is one of the weapons of our warfare that is not carnal (natural) but is mighty (supernatural) through God to the pulling down of strongholds (2 Corinthians 10:4).

God wants the Church of Jesus Christ to launch an attack against the devil's strongholds, and to pull them down. We are to cast Satan out of control in this earth. Peter said on the Day of Pentecost, *"The Lord said unto my Lord, Sit thou on my right hand, until I make thy foes thy footstool"* (Acts 2:34-35). Jesus is going to sit at the right hand of the Father until His enemies are under His feet. Who is going to do that? God said, *"Until I make thy foes thy footstool."* God, by His Spirit, Who was sent forth on the Day of Pentecost to indwell born-again, new creatures in Christ Jesus, is going to put Jesus' enemies under His feet! The last enemy that will be destroyed on the earth is death (1 Corinthians 15:25-26). The Church of Jesus Christ, by the power and control of the Holy Spirit, is going to defeat death, as well as every other enemy of God. The Bible tells us that the Church is going to overthrow Satan's control of the earth. The earth already belongs to Jesus, for He said, "All power (authority) both in heaven and in earth has been given to Me" (paraphrase).

Why has Satan stayed in control, even though he has no authority? Because the Church has been carnally minded instead of spiritually minded. God is demanding that we change.

God's Will for Man

We have a job to do. We must repossess this earth. It does not belong to Satan. God is the possessor of heaven and earth. This assignment can only be accomplished by His Spirit. God will take control of the earth when born-again, new creatures like you and me allow the Spirit of God to have control of us!

Some people misunderstand that statement. They say, "Well, God can do anything He wants to. He does not need man to control the earth. He is God."

God is God, and He can do anything He wants
to. And what He wants is for man to control the
earth through Him. Adam was to dominate and
subdue the earth by obeying God. God's dream is
for the earth to be ruled by beings created in His
image. His plan is for those who are born of Him to
rule the earth in His love and truth. These new
creatures who walk and talk and act like their Father
are to be controlled by His Holy Spirit and His love.

In dealing with man, God's stand has always
been "I want him to want Me." He has said, "Seek
Me and you will find Me. Honor Me and I will
honor you." God's desire is for man and He insists
that man's desire be for Him. This allows God to be
God in our midst. This welcomes the presence of
God in the earth. God has always desired to be in
the midst of His people. You can see this in the
Garden of Eden and in His dealings with the children
of Israel, especially in the book of Exodus. His dream
will come to pass (Revelation 21:3-7). He will dwell
among His people. The fearful, the unbelieving, the
abominable, murderers, whoremongers, sorcerers,

idolators and liars will be removed from the earth
and God will be at home here (Revelation 21:8).

Listen to the Spirit

We know the beginning and the end of God's
plan for earth. The "how to" we have to learn from
the Spirit of God. We have to learn to walk in the
spirit and we learn to do it one step at a time, just
like we learned to walk in the natural. When we
spend time praying in the spirit, we give the Holy
Spirit an opportunity to pray the perfect will of God
for our lives.

We may not have any idea what the perfect will
of God is; we therefore cannot pray effectively with
our understanding. But the Holy Spirit knows
exactly what to pray in order to get God's will done
in our lives.

**And in like manner also the Spirit lends
us a helping hand with reference to our
weakness, for the particular thing that we
should pray for according to what is**

necessary in the nature of the case, we do not know with an absolute knowledge.

(Romans 8:26, WUEST)

The Holy Spirit gives us utterance that is founded on absolute knowledge. He goes right to the root of the problem.

And He Who searches the hearts of men knows what is in the mind of the [Holy] Spirit [what His intent is], because the Spirit intercedes and pleads [before God] in behalf of the saints according to and in harmony with God's will.

(Romans 8:27, AMP)

With our limited understanding of spiritual things, often we only know the result of something wrong in our lives. The best way to explain this is with an example. You might be asking God to heal your body. You think sickness is the problem, when sometimes it is a result of something more serious. You ask God to heal you. The Holy Spirit is prompting you in your spirit, saying, *You should forgive your sister-in-law.* But you pay no attention to that prompting because the sickness in your body is so important, and your sister-in-law is far down on your list of priorities.

The Holy Spirit is going to the root. He is endeavoring to stop the problem at the source of trouble. If you receive healing but continue in sin, then another problem would occur. Unforgiveness is sin. To God, the first priority is that we walk in love. To walk in love is God's commandment to the Church.

The Holy Spirit will continue to lead you to forgive. If you determine to walk in the spirit and if you spend time praying in the spirit and seeking God's will for your life, then you will pay attention to that leading. You will obey, not even realizing that your own healing is contingent on your obedience. If you go after God and His will, you will learn to make adjustments quickly and cause your will to agree with His.

Every day as you have been believing God for the healing of your body, you have also been praying in the Holy Spirit, giving Him place and control in your life. While you have been asking for healing, which is merely a side issue, He has been praying the perfect will of God through you in this matter—that you walk in love with your sister-in-law! With your cooperation, He overcomes your weakness. You hear His voice and obey it. You forgive. You are back in agreement with God. Sickness loses its foothold. You have victory, and the Holy Spirit has you!

Let Your Spirit Speak by the Holy Spirit

For he that speaketh in an unknown tongue speaketh not unto men, but unto God: for no man understandeth him; howbeit in the spirit he speaketh mysteries.

(1 Corinthians 14:2)

A mystery is something we cannot know with our intellect. A mystery is something beyond our knowledge. Mysteries are in the realm which is described in Ephesians 3:20—a realm beyond what we can ask or think. The Bible says we know in part and we prophesy in part. We are not nearly as smart as we think we are.

If you are praying in the spirit, you are not praying "in part." When you pray in the spirit, the Holy Spirit brings the mysteries of the Father into the earth. Praying in the spirit causes the Father's perfect will to overwhelm the course of this earth. In this hour it is so critical that we pray and intercede in the spirit, because God wants to do some things in the earth that we have never even thought of, much less asked for.

Let your spirit speak by the Holy Spirit to bring into this earth the magnificent era of God's plan that He desires to manifest in these last days.

God does not do anything in the earth unless man gives Him an opportunity. If people do not pray and ask God for answers, then nothing will happen. The Spirit of God does not move in the natural realm unless people pray and use their authority in the earth. In Exodus 3:7-8 God said, *"I...have heard their cry...and I am come down to deliver them."*

Howbeit we speak wisdom among them that are perfect: yet not the wisdom of this world, nor of the princes of this world, that come to nought: But we speak the wisdom of

God in a mystery, even the hidden wisdom,
which God ordained before the world unto
our glory.

(1 Corinthians 2:6-7)

Now read verse 7 in *The Amplified Bible:*

But rather what we are setting forth is a
wisdom of God once hidden [from the human
understanding] and now revealed to us by
God—[that wisdom] which God devised and
decreed before the ages for our glorification
[to lift us into the glory of His presence].

Which none of the princes of this world
knew: for had they known it, they would not
have crucified the Lord of glory.

(verse 8, KJV)

God has a plan. He has always had a plan. He
began working His plan before the foundation of
the world, and He has never deviated from it
(Ephesians 1:4). God has a way to bring this earth
back into fellowship with Him. The Bible says God
knows how to deliver the godly out of temptation
(2 Peter 2:9). God has the way for the Church of

Jesus Christ to rise up as the glorious Church without spot or wrinkle. He reveals His plan to us as we get in the spirit. There are some things that we don't know about His plan, and there are some things we do know about it (Ephesians 1-2). But when it comes to fulfilling His plan on a day-by-day basis, we lack knowledge of the details.

The Father sent the Holy Spirit to you to lead you into all truth and to show you things to come. There is only one way you can accomplish the will of God in your life—by obeying His Spirit one day at a time.

The Holy Spirit reveals the wisdom of God to you—it is the "hidden wisdom" which God ordained before the foundation of the world (1 Corinthians 2:7). The Church's hearing and obeying the wisdom of God will remove the spots and wrinkles, so that this glorious Church will be holy and without blemish.

Pray God's Will

Since you can only do the will of God one day at a time, you need to find out every day what His

will is. *"But we speak the wisdom of God in a mystery."*
When we pray in tongues—in the spirit—we speak
mysteries. In the spirit we are decreeing the plan of
God which we do not understand or even know in
our natural minds. But because we are spiritual
beings, we trust the Word of God and we pray as
the Holy Ghost gives us utterance. We do not even
know what we are praying for, but we know it is
good, because we know that when we pray in the
spirit, we pray the perfect will of God.

If we all would start praying the will of God,
God's work would be done quickly. God would be
able to get His will done in the earth. Isn't that
what Jesus told the disciples to pray? *"Thy will be
done on earth as it is in heaven."* His will must be
prayed. In the spirit, He can use our mouths and
our authority, even if we do not mentally know
what we are saying. When we pray in the spirit, we
give Him place to display and manifest His glory
and to fulfill His plan. When we pray in the spirit,
we speak forth the mysteries of God—His hidden
plans to repossess this earth.

As we pray His will in the spirit, the Holy Spirit begins to reveal to our minds what God is doing and how we individually fit into that plan. Supernatural understanding comes to our minds as we pray in the spirit.

God knows exactly how to deliver His children. He knows how to deliver the children of God as surely as He knew how to deliver the children of Israel from the bondage of Egypt. That took some doing. Have you ever thought about how God delivered the children of Israel and read about it in such a way that you realized the Bible is not just a storybook? It really happened! Read the book of Exodus with the understanding that this is your God and your Father. The One Who lives in you did this!

When God gets ready to deliver His people, you'd better look out, Pharaoh. Pharaoh, in all his splendor and glory, had to eat dirt when God got ready to deliver His people. God knew exactly how to bring them out. And He knows exactly how to bring you and me to that place of being the glorious Church without spot or wrinkle. He knows exactly how to do it! And He is going to do it!

I get excited when I think about all of us coming before the Lord praying the mysteries of God into the earth. If we will get in the spirit, walk in the spirit, pray in the spirit and intercede in the spirit, we will bring the mysteries of God into our very presence in our lifetime. God has never told us to do anything we could not do. He has never commanded us to be spiritual beyond what He has made us able to do. Every one of us can pray in the spirit—in tongues—every day. You don't even have to be smart to pray in tongues. You just have to be full of the Holy Ghost.

The devil does not have a chance if we will just be obedient to God. When we walk in the spirit, we agree with God. If I am in agreement with God, and you are in agreement with God, we will automatically be in agreement with each other. If we will walk after the spirit, we are going to agree with each other, because we are agreeing with the Holy Spirit. By the Spirit of God, the unity of our faith becomes a reality. We are learning to agree with God in His Spirit!

God Reveals by His Spirit

But as it is written, Eye hath not seen, nor ear heard, neither have entered into the heart of man, the things which God hath prepared for them that love him. But God hath revealed them unto us by his Spirit: for the Spirit searcheth all things, yea, the deep things of God.

(1 Corinthians 2:9-10)

In our natural minds, with eyes that see physical things and ears that hear physical noises, we do not know the wonderful and exciting things God has already prepared for those who love Him. The WEYMOUTH translation says, *"All that God has in readiness for them that love Him."* The *Amplified Bible* translation defines those who love him as *"those who hold Him in affectionate reverence, promptly obeying Him and gratefully recognizing the benefits He has bestowed."*

The natural eye cannot see it, nor can the natural ear understand it. But God reveals these great things to us by His Spirit. The Holy Spirit, Who proceeds directly from the Father, reveals these deep things in our spirit by living in us and leading us into all truth.

> **For what man knoweth the things of a man, save the spirit of man which is in him? even so the things of God knoweth no man, but the Spirit of God. Now we have received, not the spirit of the world, but the spirit which is of God; that we might know the things that are freely given to us of God.**
>
> **(1 Corinthians 2:11-12)**

We have received the Spirit, which is of God, that we might know what God has freely given to us. The Holy Spirit reveals the thoughts of God to us so that we will understand our Father and walk with Him even while we live in this earth. Because God has given us His Spirit to live in us, we are able to know the Father before we go to heaven. We know, comprehend and understand Him as He reveals Himself to us by His Spirit. If you understand just a fraction of how wonderful this truth is, you will gladly give the rest of your life on earth to cultivate fellowship with the Father.

> **Which things also we speak, not in the words which man's wisdom teacheth, but which the Holy Ghost teacheth; comparing spiritual things with spiritual. But the natural man receiveth not the things of the Spirit of God: for they are foolishness unto him: neither can he know them, because they are spiritually discerned.**
>
> **(1 Corinthians 2:13-14)**

If you do not spend time in the Word of God and in prayer with God, you will not understand the words and teachings of the Holy Spirit. The wisdom of God will be foolishness to you instead of life. WEYMOUTH says,

> **Not in language which man's wisdom teaches us, but in that which the Spirit teaches, adapting spiritual words to spiritual truths. The unspiritual man rejects the teachings of the Spirit of God; to him they are**

**folly, and he cannot learn them, because they
are spiritually appraised.**

See how unlimited we are in the realm of
the spirit? People are going to think we know
everything when we really don't! But we really do
know the Spirit of God, and He knows everything!

*"But the natural man receiveth not the things of
the Spirit of God: for they are foolishness unto him."*
Natural men cannot speak in tongues. They think it
is the dumbest thing they have ever heard. They do
not receive the things of the Spirit of God. Yet, on
the other hand, natural men are desperate. They
don't have any answers. They don't know what to
do next. If you will begin to live the life of the Spirit
in front of them, they will see God in your life.
They will begin to say, "This is what I need. I must
have this. I must have this life of God in me. Those
people are different. They are so full of joy and they
walk in love. I must have this." Even though the
things of God look foolish to the world, your
peaceful life will look so desirable that others will
come to you to find out how to walk in the power
of God.

The Bible says that if you pray in an unknown tongue, you should pray for the interpretation (1 Corinthians 14:14-15). These scriptures are speaking about interpreting before the congregation, but I believe we can also expect an interpretation in our private devotions. You have probably been doing it without realizing it. In our private prayer time, many times we pray in tongues and then pray the interpretation in English without realizing we are praying both in tongues and in English out of our spirit. Just learn to follow the Holy Spirit and flow with Him. He is the teacher!

The same Holy Spirit that prays the will of God through you in tongues can pray the will of God through you in English if you will interpret it. That interpretation will come out of your spirit—not your mind—in the language of the Holy Ghost, comparing spiritual things with spiritual.

As you spend time daily praying in the spirit, it becomes easier for you to hear the direction of the Holy Spirit as He reveals His will to your spirit.

"So now we serve not under [obedience to] the old code of written regulations, but [under obedience to the promptings] of the Spirit in newness [of life]" (Romans 7:6, AMP). We are no longer bound to obey written regulations, but we are still to serve obediently. We are to serve by obeying the promptings of our reborn spirit, which is controlled by the Holy Spirit.

The Holy Spirit communicates with your spirit. He dwells in your spirit. I believe this is an area of confusion when you are learning to walk in the spirit.

Learn to Listen

Most serious Christians would do anything God told them to if they knew for sure God's direction— if they heard Him with their natural ears or saw Him with their natural eyes. But most of the time God does not deal with you that way. He sent His Spirit to live in your spirit to constantly teach, enlighten and guide you. You must learn how to hear God in your spirit.

I have asked believers all over the world this question: When you think God may be directing you, do you say, *Was that me, Lord, or was that You?* I believe this uncertainty to be the major drawback to our following God through our spirit directed by the Holy Spirit.

I believe this will help you. As the Lord was clarifying this to me, He made me realize that most of the time I would hear my own spirit speaking to my soul, which is my mind, my will and my emotions. There is the audible voice of the Lord, but that is all too rare in most of our lives. Almost every leading you will receive in your everyday life will be a prompting, an impression, a thought, an inward witness, a leading or an unction from your spirit.

The reason it sounds like you is because it *is* you that you hear. The Holy Spirit communicates with your spirit, and your spirit prompts, or enlightens, your mind. *"But the person who is united to the Lord becomes one spirit with Him"* (1 Corinthians 6:17, AMP). The key word *united* in Greek means "to glue or cement together." Jesus said, *"If a man love me, he will keep my words: and my Father will love him, and*

we will come unto him, and make our abode with him"
(John 14:23). This describes being joined, or
united, to the Lord.

When you start your day by praying the will of
God by the Holy Spirit, many times you will have
already prayed concerning the problems you will face
during the day. You will perceive an interpretation,
a prompting, an impression, a word or a sentence
that will enlighten you and give you the answer to
the situation. It will be so natural to you that you
might not even realize it was the Holy Spirit leading
and revealing Himself to you. Things that would
have been stumbling blocks to you before now will
be handled with ease by hearing and obeying the
will of God as the Holy Spirit leads you.

You need to learn to instantly obey the voice
of your spirit. I don't think there is any way to
cultivate this communion between the Holy Spirit
and your spirit, and between your spirit and your
mind, except by spending time in prayer and in the
Word of God.

We read that the Holy Spirit teaches by comparing spiritual things with spiritual. Hebrews 4:12 says, *"For the word of God is quick, and powerful, and sharper than any twoedged sword, piercing even to the dividing asunder of soul and spirit."*

The Word of God is the only thing that will separate or differentiate between the soul and the spirit. Your soul relies on natural knowledge to form its opinions until natural knowledge is replaced by the supernatural knowledge of God. In Romans 12:2, this process of replacing the thoughts of natural, carnal man with the thoughts of God is called "the renewing of the mind."

You might be asking, "How can I tell the difference and be sure when it is God or just me?" You will have to begin a quest for the things of God. The Scripture lets us know that if we seek God, we will find Him. Spiritual things do not come without serious effort. We are told in Hebrews 11:6 that *"without faith it is impossible to please him: for he that cometh to [God] must believe that he is, and that he is a rewarder of them that diligently seek him."* We know that we have to approach God in faith—that is, without being able to see proof in the natural realm. You will never be able to put spiritual things in a test tube. You will have to learn to walk without evidence in the seen realm. We must learn to believe Him without seeing Him. From that verse we also find another key to knowing God: He is the rewarder of those who diligently seek Him. Lazy Christians never mature spiritually, because diligence is required to develop in God.

I cannot teach you how to walk in the spirit in seven easy steps. I can only point the way and share with you truths I have learned which are working in my life. I am still learning, myself. There is no selfish, easy way to walk with God while you live in the earth and in a natural body. You will do it God's way or you will not do it at all. His way is for us to serve Him with our whole spirit, soul and body.

You must allow Him to be God in your life if you want to walk in the spirit. We have to change our thoughts, opinions and actions to agree with His. We have to mature spiritually day by day. God wants us to live the rest of our time in this earth, not conforming to the will of man, not to our own will, but conforming to His will. When we put ourselves in a position of obedience, we give God the freedom to overwhelm the natural circumstances of this life with His supernatural power.

To the degree that we disagree with God, we diminish the presence of God in our lives.

To the degree that we agree with God, we welcome the presence of God in our lives.

Grow Up!

Your born-again spirit, led by the Holy Spirit, should have a place of dictatorship over your being. Your spirit is re-created in Christ Jesus to rule over your soul (mind) and your body (flesh).

As you learn by experience to walk in the spirit, remember God's Word comes to us in two ways: (1) by the written Word, and (2) by the Holy Spirit speaking to our spirit. We begin with the assurance that God's written Word is our sure word. The Holy Spirit will never lead you contrary to the written

Word of God. If you receive a prompting that is in opposition to the written Word, you will know it is not from the Holy Spirit.

Simply ask the Holy Spirit to teach you how to follow Him. Give Him control of your life and He will reveal to you the will of God, step by step. He knows how to bring you to maturity. All He requires of you is your attention and your obedience.

> **And let the peace (soul harmony which comes) from Christ rule (act as umpire continually) in your hearts [deciding and settling with finality all questions that arise in your minds, in that peaceful state] to which as [members of Christ's] one body you were also called [to live]. And be thankful (appreciative), [giving praise to God always].**
>
> **(Colossians 3:15, AMP)**

This was one of the first verses the Lord revealed to me years ago concerning making a decision. Let peace be your umpire! I have learned to check my heart for peace. If I am agitated in my spirit about something, I don't do anything until that changes. Before I take action, I wait until I have peace in my spirit. Continue to inquire of the Lord until you KNOW.

Another scripture that helped me was Proverbs 16:3:

> **Roll your works upon the Lord [commit and trust them wholly to Him; He will cause your thoughts to become agreeable to His will, and] so shall your plans be established and succeed.**

> **I roll my works upon the Lord and expect my thoughts to become agreeable to His will. I expect Him to energize in me the power and desire to will and to work for His good pleasure, satisfaction and delight.**
>
> **(See Philippians 2:13, AMP)**

"Trust in the Lord with all thine heart; and lean not unto thine own understanding. In all thy ways acknowledge him, and he shall direct thy paths. Be not wise in thine own eyes: fear the Lord, and depart from evil" (Proverbs 3:5-7). This is also a vital scripture on receiving direction. These three verses helped me as I was maturing in the Lord. God was so faithful

to reveal these simple instructions to me early in my Christian walk.

He will not tell you to part the Red Sea the first day you begin to walk as a Christian! You will start where you are. If you are a baby Christian and have not grown spiritually, you will start in kindergarten! (If you do not look just like Jesus, you are not fully grown.)

The Holy Spirit will begin to reveal areas in your own life that need to be corrected. He will not send you on some world-changing errand. But He will begin to lead you to mortify the deeds of your body so you can begin to live in the power of God. Romans 8:13-14 tells us this: *"but if ye through the Spirit do mortify the deeds of the body, ye shall live. For as many as are led by the Spirit of God, they are the sons of God."* Children of God grow up to be mature sons and daughters by obeying the Holy Spirit concerning their own lives.

All along, you probably have been receiving direction from the Holy Spirit, telling you that you need to make certain changes in your life. But many times Christians are not too interested in hearing God deal with them on this level—not realizing that this is where walking in the spirit begins. They want to hear something BIG from the Holy Spirit, like "Go to China." If you do not follow the Holy Spirit in the area of correcting your own life, you would be of little value to God when you got to China!

Many times we are like Peter was in the Garden of Gethsemane. He was willing to die for Jesus. He was willing to go to jail! He was ready to do something big and important. ANYTHING! NOTHING WOULD HAVE BEEN TOO GREAT!

Jesus said, *"Watch and pray."* *No, Lord, that is not what I had in mind.* Peter did not follow Jesus' will in something simple. Jesus wanted him to pray so that when temptations came he would overcome them.

Peter did not follow God in praying, and when the pressure came, he did not follow God in action. He suffered a major defeat.

Jesus did not want him to die. He did not want
him to go to jail. He did not want him to go to
China. He wanted him to pray!

There is no leading from the Holy Spirit that is
insignificant. If it is from God, it is priority. We
should have this attitude of meekness: Father, there
is nothing too great or too small. Reveal Your will
to me and I will do it.

Doers of the Word

**Wherefore lay apart all filthiness and
superfluity of naughtiness, and receive with
meekness the engrafted word, which is able
to save your souls. But be ye doers of the
word, and not hearers only, deceiving your
own selves.**

(James 1:21-22)

The implanted Word received with meekness
is able to save your soul (your mind, will and
emotions). Remember that the Word of God
separates the soul from the spirit. The Word of God

received with meekness causes your soul to agree with your spirit as it is led by the Holy Spirit. First Peter 1:22 says you purify your soul in obeying the truth through the Spirit.

To receive the word *"with meekness"* means that when the Word is revealed to us, we must adapt ourselves or our lives to obey that Word. We are to be doers of the Word. When we only hear the Word, but fail to do it, we deceive ourselves. We cannot walk in the spirit by the Holy Spirit unless we obey God's Word.

Do you want to be self-deceived or do you want to walk as a child of light? Will you spend time in prayer and in the Word, or will you spend time in the pleasures of this world? No one can make these decisions for you.

Watch and Pray

Jesus lived above the weakness of His flesh by walking in the spirit. He gave us spiritual insight that enables us to do the same. *"Pray, lest ye enter into temptation"* (Luke 22:46). He said in Luke 21:35-36:

> **For as a snare shall it come on all them that dwell on the face of the whole earth. Watch ye therefore, and pray always, that ye may be accounted worthy to escape all these things that shall come to pass, and to stand before the Son of man.**

The way to escape the evil in this world is to "watch and pray."

WUEST says, *"But be circumspect, attentive, ready, in every season being in prayer, in order that you may have sufficient strength to be escaping all these things...."*

At the Garden of Gethsemane, it was not in Peter's heart to fail God. If he had prayed, he probably would not have failed Him; and when temptation came, he would not have entered into it.

What is in your heart? Do you want to walk free from sin? Do you want to please God? Do you want to be a stalwart believer, one on whom God can depend and one whom God counts faithful? If so, your heart's desire is to be a wise and faithful servant.

As we pray in the spirit, the Spirit of God takes what is in our hearts and manifests God's perfect will in our lives. Praying in the spirit brings the will of our hearts to pass. It causes the will of the spirit to dominate the will of the flesh. It gives our spirit control over our flesh.

The key is prayer. Give a tithe of your time to the Lord. Daily spend an hour praying in the spirit and an hour in the Word and your life will be changed.

Listen to the counsel of the Holy Spirit every moment and obey His promptings. It will cause the spirit realm to become a reality to you. Give the Holy Spirit control of your life. You will begin to walk in the spirit instead of after the flesh.

A Living Sacrifice

"I beseech you therefore, brethren, by the mercies of God, that ye present your bodies a living sacrifice, holy, acceptable unto God, Which is your reasonable service."

Romans 12:1

CHAPTER 4

A Living Sacrifice

Harvest time is here! This wave of glory is to harvest the souls of this earth into the kingdom of God.

We must exercise as much diligence toward learning to walk in the spirit as we have used learning to walk by faith. The glory of God will not be manifested in a Church that is slothful and unspiritual. If we are too busy serving our own desires to seek the Lord and listen to His voice, this move of the Spirit will simply pass us by. He wants to show us things to come. He wants to show us how to walk in His glory! It's time to walk in the realm of the supernatural.

The role of the Holy Spirit is to manifest the presence of Jesus in the Body of Christ. He is in us to bring forth the image of Jesus. The things that hinder Him are our carnal thinking and carnal ways. God does not want us to be conformed to the world. He wants us to be transformed by renewing our minds to think and act like Him. God is calling us to function in the realm of the spirit.

The manifestation of God's power in the Church is directly related to the holiness in the Body. God does not manifest Himself when His people are disobedient and have sin in their lives. If we don't lay aside the things of the world and give our attention to spiritual things, we will never be able to walk in the glory that God wants to reveal in us. We must be willing to change our attitudes and our priorities to please the Father.

The Holy Spirit works in us to bring our consciousness, or awareness, into the realm of the spirit. Satan works without to keep us bound to this world.

Second Timothy 2:21 says that if a man will purge himself of iniquity, he will be a vessel of honor, prepared for every good work. Notice who does the purging. The man himself!

> And what agreement hath the temple of God with idols? for ye are the temple of the living God; as God hath said, I will dwell in them, and walk in them; and I will be their God, and they shall be my people.... Having therefore these promises, dearly beloved, let us cleanse ourselves from all filthiness of the flesh and spirit, perfecting holiness in the fear of God.
>
> (2 Corinthians 6:16, 7:1)

Do Not Be Drawn Away

> Let no man say when he is tempted, I am tempted of God: for God cannot be tempted with evil, neither tempteth he any man: But every man is tempted, when he is drawn away of his own lust, and enticed. Then when lust

hath conceived, it bringeth forth sin: and sin,
when it is finished, bringeth forth death.

(James 1:13-15)

This scripture says we are tempted when we are drawn away. Drawn away from what? From God. As new creatures in Christ Jesus, our inner man wants to do the will of God. Our hearts want to please Him and to do what is right in His sight. We, however, have to contend with the temptations of the flesh.

The word most often associated with *flesh* is the term "lust." In our thinking it is connected with sex or immorality. But in the Greek, the word simply means "strong desire." The lust of the flesh is simply the strong desire to follow after the ways of the world, rather than after God. For instance, a lust for money can pull you away from God.

It is acceptable to have a desire for success, or to obtain an education or career, or even to be recognized in your profession. These "wants" are permissible if they are kept in perspective—behind God. But we must always be watchful that these things do not draw us away from God, and that we follow God's will for our lives. Our strong desire must be for God.

The Father wants us to be successful. On the other hand, Jesus said, "What does it profit a man if he gains the whole world and loses his own soul?"

We do not want to be drawn away from God through fleshly desires. We can walk and function in this world without being of it (John 17:16). As believers, we are already citizens of the kingdom of heaven. We are not of this world.

Be Sensitive to the Holy Spirit

In the past we were debtors to the flesh. But now God is calling us to set our affection on things above. He wants us to give our attention to the things of the spirit so we can dominate the world around us with the love and power of God. God has patiently waited for the Church. It is time for His power and glory to be manifested as it has never been before.

The Lord told Kenneth that there are three things we would have to do to move in the flow of the Holy Spirit: 1) We must purge ourselves of sin; 2) we must intercede; and 3) we must prepare for criticism.

> **But if the Spirit of him that raised up Jesus from the dead dwell in you, he that raised up Christ from the dead shall also quicken your mortal bodies by his Spirit that dwelleth in you. Therefore, brethren, we are debtors, not to the flesh, to live after the flesh. For if ye live after the flesh, ye shall die: but if ye through the Spirit do mortify the deeds of the body, ye shall live. For as many as are led by the Spirit of God, they are the sons of God.**
>
> **(Romans 8:11-14)**

In the Old Testament God's children were very careful about the dwelling place of the Spirit of God. We must consider Who is living in us! We are walking, mobile temples of the Holy Ghost! "I will be a Father to them," God said. "I will dwell in them and walk in them."

The same Spirit that raised Jesus from the dead will raise you from the bondage of a mortal body. He quickened the mortal flesh of Jesus and He will quicken our mortal flesh by His Spirit. But we have to give Him place. You must be sensitive to Him and be ever conscious of His presence.

The Holy Spirit is not a dictator. He will move only when you yield to Him. He is our strengthener. He is the One called alongside to help. He cannot assist us if we will not participate with Him in spiritual action. We must be aware of His presence and cooperate with Him.

Offer Yourself

I beseech you therefore, brethren, by the mercies of God, that ye present your bodies a living sacrifice, holy, acceptable unto God, which is your reasonable service. And be not conformed to this world: but be ye transformed by the renewing of your mind,

that ye may prove what is that good, and
acceptable, and perfect, will of God.

(Romans 12:1-2)

This scripture in Romans 12 is talking about
crucifying the flesh, as is Galatians 5:24-25: *"And
they that are Christ's have crucified the flesh with the
affections and lusts. If we live in the Spirit, let us also
walk in the Spirit."* We are admonished to offer our
bodies as living sacrifices. We are to lay aside our
own natural desires in order to fulfill God's desires.
WUEST says that we are to place our bodies at the
disposal of God.

According to the Bible, this is only our reasonable
service, although it might seem an unreasonable
demand to some. Why is it our reasonable service?
Because Jesus gave His body as a living sacrifice for
us. We have been bought with a price, and we are
to glorify God in our bodies and in our spirit
(1 Corinthians 6:19-20).

The Greek word translated *Lord* means "master"
or "owner." Jesus became your new owner the
moment you made Him the Lord of your life. Most

Christians get born again but will not allow Jesus to be Lord in their lives. They choose to continue to walk in the darkness of this world, when they could walk in the light of God.

"[The Father] has delivered and drawn us to Himself out of the control and the dominion of darkness and has transferred us into the kingdom of the Son of His love" (Colossians 1:13, AMP). We have been transferred into the kingdom of God. We are to place our bodies and our minds at the disposal of God and allow the Holy Spirit to teach us how to live under the dominion of God.

This sacrifice of our body is to be a holy and well-pleasing (acceptable) sacrifice. The Greek word *thusia,* translated sacrifice, denotes "the act of offering." We are to make an offering of our bodies. You are the offering that God desires.

What does God desire of us as a continual offering unto Him? He desires that our bodies not conform to, or be fashioned after, this world, which is patterned after Satan. He wants our bodies at His disposal so He can change them from worldliness to godliness. We are to be transformed by the renewing of our minds. W. E. Vine says the word *renew* means "the adjustment of the moral and spiritual vision and thinking to the mind of God." We are to adjust our thinking to the mind of God. The Holy Spirit teaches us to think like God thinks and to act like God acts. As we do this, the outward expression of our body will begin to match the inward expression of Jesus. We will begin to walk in the good and well-pleasing and perfect will of God.

Offer yourself as a living sacrifice. Lay down your own desires in order to fulfill God's desire. This is not an unreasonable thing for God to ask. This is only your reasonable service, because you have been bought with a precious price. Jesus purchased you with the crucifying of His own flesh, and He shed His blood to redeem you. Jesus became a living sacrifice for you. The least you can do is give your body to God, for you are not your own.

There is a decision to be made. Are you going to serve your own interests or are you going to serve the Lord Jesus? I believe you are going to decide to offer yourself as a living sacrifice. And when you do, you are going to find that you do not have to fight the war between your flesh and your spirit. Your spirit, controlled by the Holy Spirit, will stop the war! As you obey the Holy Spirit, the law of the Spirit of life that is in Christ Jesus will make you free from the law of sin and death.

Train Your Flesh to Obey

Before you experienced the new birth, your body was trained to enforce evil practices. You were dominated by outward influences. As you yield yourself more and more to God, you retrain your flesh to enforce the things of God (Romans 6:16-23).

For every one that useth milk is unskilful in the word of righteousness: for he is a babe. But strong meat belongeth to them that are of full age, even those who by reason of use [or through practice] have their senses [bodies] exercised to discern both good and evil.

(Hebrews 5:13-14)

It isn't easy at first, but through practice, your body will discern the difference between good and evil. It is not something you have to fight. If you will walk in the spirit, when temptation comes, the Holy Spirit will lead you to mortify the deeds of the body and you will resist that temptation. You will find that the more you walk in the spirit, the more your body is affected and brought under obedience to God.

The Spirit of God will have an effect on your natural body. Proverbs 4:20-22 substantiates this. It says the Word of God is *"life to those that find them and health to all their flesh."*

"The Word of God is quick [alive], powerful, and sharper than any twoedged sword" (Hebrews 4:12). God's Spirit is in His Word. It will bring health to your body. The Word of God and the Spirit of God will quicken your flesh. Jesus said, *"My words are spirit and they are life."*

"Keep thy heart with all diligence; for out of it are the issues [forces] of life" (Proverbs 4:23). As they are released through your will, these issues, or forces, of

the reborn spirit crucify the desires of the flesh and demand that it obey God. These forces are love, joy, peace, longsuffering, gentleness, goodness, faith, meekness and temperance (Galatians 5:22-23). Doesn't love affect your flesh? And doesn't joy? If you have peace, doesn't it benefit you physically? The issues of the spirit will quicken your mortal flesh and train your flesh to enforce the things of God and not reject them.

Once we have given ourselves totally to God, how do we get to the place where our spirit is the dominating force? I believe 1 Peter 4:1-2 is speaking very directly to us today. It says:

> **So, since Christ suffered in the flesh for us, for you, arm yourselves with the same thought and purpose [patiently to suffer rather than fail to please God]. For whoever has suffered in the flesh [having the mind of Christ] is done with [intentional] sin [has stopped pleasing himself and the world, and pleases God], So that he can no longer spend the rest of his natural life living by [his]**

human appetites and desires, but [he lives] for what God wills (AMP).

As believers, we are called to enter into the sufferings of Jesus (1 Peter 4:13). Religious tradition has taught that these sufferings are trials, sickness, disease, poverty, etc. The Bible says Jesus was our substitute. When He paid the price for sin, He redeemed us from all the curse of the law (Galatians 3:13; Deuteronomy 28:15-68).

Arm yourselves with this thought: *I will suffer in the flesh rather than fail to please God.* Thinking this way releases the Holy Spirit to strengthen and to empower us to overcome. Our will releases Him to impart Himself to us. It is a decision of whether we are going to please ourselves or please the Father. *"For whoever has suffered in the flesh has ceased from sin."* That person has stopped pleasing himself and the world so he might please God. And that's what God is calling us to do. He is asking us to give ourselves. He is asking us to serve.

"If any man serve me, let him follow me; and where I am, there shall also my servant be: if any man serve

me, him will my Father honour" (John 12:26). Jesus said, "If any man serves Me, him will the Father honor." You cannot serve yourself and your own interests, and serve Jesus at the same time. You have to make a decision, "Who am I going to serve? Am I going to serve my own interests and go after the natural things that are in the world—after my natural desires? Or am I going to serve the Lord Jesus, Who bought me?"

"For he that hath suffered in the flesh hath ceased from sin; That he no longer should live the rest of his time in the flesh to the lusts of men, but to the will of God" (1 Peter 4:1-2). And that's where we want to live—in the will of God.

To enter into His sufferings simply means to give up the desires of the flesh in order to walk in the spirit. Jesus said, *"If any man will come after me, let him deny himself, and take up his cross, and follow me"* (Matthew 16:24). It would be accurate to say, "let him deny his flesh," or "let him deny selfishness." Taking up our cross is denying ourselves the luxury of walking after the flesh. We must disregard our own interests and desires in order to walk in the spirit. God must be allowed to be Lord of our lives.

Jesus suffered in that He came to the earth and lived in a natural body just like yours and mine. He was tempted by the weakness of the flesh, yet He never sinned. Jesus suffered through His obedience.

For verily he took not on him the nature of angels; but he took on him the seed of Abraham. Wherefore in all things it behooved him to be made like unto his brethren, that he might be a merciful and faithful high priest in things pertaining to God, to make reconciliation for the sins of the people. For in that he himself hath suffered being tempted, he is able to succour them that are tempted.

(Hebrews 2:16-18)

We are tempted in the flesh. That is the way we suffer. That is the way Jesus suffered when He was living on the earth.

We are to suffer the crucifying of our flesh and bring it into obedience to God so that God's glory can be revealed in us.

The little suffering we do by commanding our flesh to be obedient is nothing compared to the glory that will be revealed in us (Romans 8:18). We are only giving up the things in this life that work death in us. The wages of sin is death and the gift of God is life. Death has no sting when it has been swallowed up in life. First Corinthians 15:56 reveals that sin is the sting of death. Sin gives death its place.

Then cometh the end, when he shall have delivered up the kingdom to God, even the Father; when he shall have put down all rule and all authority and power. For he must reign, till he hath put all enemies under his feet. The last enemy that shall be destroyed is death.

(1 Corinthians 15:24-26)

"But insofar as you are sharing Christ's sufferings, rejoice, so that when His glory [full of radiance and splendor] is revealed, you may also rejoice with triumph

[exultantly]" (1 Peter 4:13, AMP). God wants to reveal His glory in you.

God wants us to crucify the flesh, or mortify the deeds of the body, by His Spirit. He has put His Spirit in us to cause us to walk in His ways (Ezekiel 36:27). Peter says, *"Suffer in the flesh."* The word *suffer* in Greek means "to die." These scriptures are all saying the same thing: We are to render our flesh obedient to God so we might know, or experience, Him and the power of His resurrection.

> [For my determined purpose is] that I may know Him [that I may progressively become more deeply and intimately acquainted with Him, perceiving and recognizing and understanding the wonders of His Person more strongly and more clearly], and that I may in that same way come to know the power outflowing from His resurrection [which it exerts over believers], and that I may so share His sufferings as to be continually transformed [in spirit into His likeness even] to His death, [in the hope] That if possible I may attain to the [spiritual

and moral] resurrection [that lifts me] out from among the dead [even while in the body]. So let those [of us] who are spiritually mature and full-grown have this mind and hold these convictions; and if in any respect you have a different attitude of mind, God will make that clear to you also.

(Philippians 3:10-11, 15, AMP)

In verse 15 Paul said, "So let us who are spiritually mature and full grown have this mind and hold these convictions."

The manifestation of the glory of God in our lives depends on our bringing our flesh under subjection. If you don't have control over your flesh, then the Holy Spirit does not have control over your flesh.

For if ye live after the flesh, ye shall die: but if ye through the Spirit do mortify the deeds of the body, ye shall live. For ye have not received the spirit of bondage again to fear; but ye have received the Spirit of adoption, whereby we cry, Abba, Father. The Spirit itself beareth witness with our spirit,

that we are the children of God: And if
children, then heirs; heirs of God, and joint-
heirs with Christ; if so be that we suffer with
him, that we may be also glorified together.
For I reckon that the sufferings of this present
time are not worthy to be compared with the
glory which shall be revealed in us.

(Romans 8:13, 15-18)

The Holy Spirit leads you to mortify the deeds of
your body. As many as obey will grow up to be the
full grown, or mature, sons of God. By mortifying
the deeds of the body through the Spirit, we can live
the life of God right here in the earth. Jesus said the
kingdom of heaven is within you. We can live that
high life that Jesus spoke about. We can live in a
position for the Spirit of God to flow through us to
the world and reveal Him to them. That is our calling.

Transformed Into His Image

*"For whom he did foreknow, he also did predestinate
to be conformed to the image of his Son, that he might
be the firstborn among many brethren"* (Romans 8:29).

You will not be squeezed into the mold of
this world. You will look and act just like Jesus!
Allow the Holy Spirit to so affect you that you
live right here on earth as if you were already in
heaven. Heaven has no sin, sickness or lack! You
have the unlimited realm of the spirit right on
the inside of you. God dwells in you and walks in
you. God wants His Body to be vessels of His
glory manifested to the whole world.

**For God, who commanded the light to
shine out of darkness, hath shined in our
hearts, to give the light of the knowledge of
the glory of God in the face of Jesus Christ.
But we have this treasure in earthen vessels,
that the excellency of the power may be of
God, and not of us.**

(2 Corinthians 4:6-7)

God wants the Church to be transformed into
the image of Jesus. He wants us to control and
dominate the physical world around us. When your
body is presented as a living sacrifice, then God will
be revealed in you.

Today is the day! Before you do another thing, put this book down and lift your hands to God. Make your body a living sacrifice, holy and acceptable to Him. You will never be the same!

You Must Stir Yourself Up

"As truly as I live, all the earth shall
be filled with the glory of the Lord."

Numbers 14:21

You Must Stir Yourself Up

"*And they that are Christ's have crucified the flesh with the affections and lusts. If we live in the Spirit, let us also walk in the Spirit*" (Galatians 5:24-25). We cannot afford to let spiritual things get away from us. We hear the Word. We get determined. We get "on fire." We get dedicated. We must learn to maintain that zeal. Praying in the spirit and spending time with the Father will keep you dedicated. It will keep that fire burning on the inside of you. It will keep you moving in the right direction—toward God.

I have learned something I want to share with you. Ken and I have been in this a long time. When we first heard the message of faith, we were so on fire for God that nothing else in the world was of interest to us. We knew that the revelation of the integrity of God's Word was what we had been looking for in our Christian life. We learned we could depend on the Word of God the same way we would depend on the word of a trusted friend. We learned we could depend on the written Word that said, "By His stripes you are healed," just the same way, with the same expectation as if Jesus appeared to us in the flesh and called us by name.

We became so hungry to find out what God's Word says that we totally sold out to the Word of God. We did not have time for anything else. I had two small children. Kellie was 3 and John was about 9 months old. I took care of my children and my husband and studied the Word. I did not go shopping. (I did not have any money to spend anyway. I had to pray in tongues to pay for what was in my grocery basket.) I was not doing a lot of other things, but that did not matter to me. I did not care. There was nothing else as exciting to me as the Word of the living God. I was doing what I wanted to do.

Ken had begun to go preach at meetings, and sometimes he would be gone for three weeks at a time. He had to have long meetings because it would be two and a half weeks before anybody would find out he was in town. After that, it would be only a three-day meeting! Nobody knew who he was and nobody cared. He would start with a few people and build. He might even have 200 people. In big meetings he might have 300 by the end of three weeks. He would teach two services a day for 21 days.

In the beginning, we didn't have the money for me to go, so I stayed at home with the children. I must tell you, I was in one of the biggest revivals the world has ever seen and I was all by myself. Other than to care for my family, I didn't do anything except spend time in the Word. I was so hungry for God and so hungry for His Word. Night and day I would spend time in God's Word.

I read God's Word, I listened to tapes and I read books I had found about God's Word. I was dedicated. I hardly thought about anything else. My total interest was in the Word of God.

But after a few years I began to lose the strong desire I'd had at first. I think that happens to many people. It has happened to many who have started to walk by faith. It may have even happened to you. When you first find the reality of the Word, you are just naturally excited. It is such good news that you don't want to do anything else. Your desires go in God's direction without effort.

But after a time it becomes easier to be drawn away. You can begin to allow yourself to grow cold. You don't have to, but many do. You can get interested in other things and lose your desire and hunger for the Word of God. Revelation does not come as quickly to you anymore. You begin to think, *I already know all that.* The Word does not seem as exciting. This happened to me. I lost the enthusiasm for the Word that I had once enjoyed.

I didn't realize it because I was a disciplined person and had continued to make myself spend time in the Word. I had learned enough to know I could not live healed and blessed without the Word of God. I still studied the Word, but I was not hungry and excited about it as I had been at one time.

The prophecy that I heard in 1977 was word from the Lord that corrected me, instructed me and chastened me (2 Timothy 3:16-17; Hebrews 12). By the Holy Spirit, the preacher began to talk about the great and mighty army of the Lord. He said, *"Men upon this earth shall walk and talk and act like God. For they'll live in the power of God, motivated by His power, motivated by His Spirit."* At the end, the prophet of God said: *"In fact, many of those here tonight are a part of that army. You can be one if you so desire. Purpose in your heart that you will not be lazy, that you will not draw back, hold back or sit down. But purpose in your heart that you will rise up and march forward and become on fire."*

As he was speaking by inspiration of the Spirit, I thought, *You know, that has happened to me. I'm not hungry for God like I used to be. I am more interested in other things. I have to make myself spend time in God's Word.*

At one time in my life, I didn't care about anything else. I wanted to spend my time in the Word of God. I don't think I had realized I had begun to cool off until the Holy Spirit spoke to me that night.

It pays to be honest with God. When the Word of God comes to correct you, if you're not honest with yourself and with God, you are never going to grow up spiritually. When the Word of God comes to you to chasten you and it cuts into your heart, don't start making excuses. Don't start saying, "Well, I'm really not that way." Be honest. Allow the Holy Spirit to just open up your heart and show you what needs to be changed. Plead guilty and take the necessary action to change it.

I thought, *You know, I've let myself get lukewarm.* I was not doing anything as far as recognized sin. I was just not where I should be spiritually. You can go through the motions, but that is not what God wants. He wants the affection of your heart! All of you—spirit, soul and body!

The spirit is the part of you that is reborn and made into the image of God. Your soul is your mind, your will and your emotions. First Peter 1:22 says your soul is purified in obeying the truth through the spirit. Hebrews 4:12 says the Word of God is sharper than a two-edged sword, dividing asunder between soul and spirit. That is what happened to me.

You have to be willing to allow the Holy Spirit to change you to be in agreement with God. The Spirit of God changed my mind, my will and my emotions to stop following after natural things with my attention, and to immediately turn my attention to the things of God.

Your soul's desire will go after whatever you spend your time doing. I can prove this to you with something natural. If you're a golfer, you may go for months at a time without even thinking about it if you don't play for a while. But once you start playing again, your desire for it comes back. That is the way it is with anything in the natural world, and it is the same way in the spiritual world.

If you quit praying and spending time in the Word of God, your desire for the things of God will get weaker and weaker. Whatever you are doing instead of spending time with God is what you will desire. Whatever you give your attention to is the direction your desire will take. Desire follows attention, whether it is something good or something bad. It might just be a hobby that's perfectly all right for us to have. But it is not all right for us to desire that natural thing more than we desire the things of God.

You want to keep your heart and soul with fervent desire for the things of God. You must do that. I cannot do it for you. Remember that what you give your attention to determines your desire. Your motivation follows your attention.

I was working for God, but my heart, my affection (soul), and my attention were somewhere else. God wants all of you.

I believe Revelation 3:14-22 was what the Spirit of God was saying to me that night:

> And unto the angel of the church of the Laodiceans write; These things saith the Amen, the faithful and true witness, the beginning of the creation of God; I know thy works, that thou art neither cold nor hot: I would thou wert cold or hot. So then because thou art lukewarm, and neither cold nor hot, I will spew thee out of my mouth. Because thou sayest, I am rich, and increased with goods, and have need of nothing; and knowest not that thou art wretched, and miserable, and poor, and blind, and naked: I counsel thee to buy of me gold tried in the fire, that thou mayest be rich; and white raiment, that thou mayest be clothed, and that the shame of thy nakedness do not appear; and anoint thine eyes with eyesalve, that thou mayest see. As many as I love, I rebuke and chasten: be zealous therefore, and repent. Behold, I stand at the door, and knock: if any man hear my voice, and open the door, I will come in to him, and will sup

with him, and he with me. To him that overcometh will I grant to sit with me in my throne, even as I also overcame, and am set down with my Father in his throne. He that hath an ear, let him hear what the Spirit saith unto the churches.

In my soul I thought I had need of nothing, while in my spirit I was appearing wretched, miserable, poor, blind and naked. Only the Word of God will be enough to clarify and divide between the two.

The Scripture says to delight yourself in the Lord and He will give you the desires of your heart. I read that as saying, "You delight yourself in the Lord and the things that you really want in your heart, He'll give you." But I believe the depth of the meaning in that scripture is, "Delight yourself in the Lord and the desire that you have in your heart will be of God." That is what we want. We want our desires to be for Him. That is the high life!

I realized my condition, and I determined to do something about it. This word from the Lord said,

"Rise up. March forward. Become on fire. Don't be lazy. Don't hold back, and don't draw back." I had enough spiritual understanding to know that what I needed to do was to rise up spiritually, spend more time in the Word, and spend more time going after the things of God. I began to do just that. I dropped things in my life that were stealing my time, and I put my attention on the things of God, where it should have been all the time.

It took awhile to get that fire back into my heart. It took awhile to get back my strong desire for God rather than for natural things.

If you are in that condition today, it might help you to know that you are not the only one this has happened to. Everybody has opportunity to lose that fervent desire for God. If you don't keep yourself on fire, you will begin to cool off. If you let yourself go long enough in that condition, you will get in trouble.

If I had not listened to the Holy Spirit and allowed that word to correct me when the word of

God came from the prophet, I would have continued to get colder and colder.

Jesus is not fond of someone's being lukewarm. He said, "If you are lukewarm, I'll spew you out of My mouth. I'd rather you be hot or cold" (paraphrase). Being lukewarm is disgusting to Him. Why? Because, if you're lukewarm, it means you have had something offered to you by the Holy Spirit but you would not receive it. Otherwise, you wouldn't be warm at all.

If you are lukewarm, you have received some Word and some knowledge. You have had the Spirit of God dealing with you, or you wouldn't be lukewarm. If you are lukewarm, you have had an opportunity to become on fire. That is what is disgusting about being lukewarm.

We do not have to be that way. It is up to you and me. It is our choice to make whether we go on and march forward, whether we rise up and become on fire, or whether we stay lukewarm and eventually get cold. This is not the day and the hour to be a lukewarm Christian. We are at a time when the power of God is going to be manifested. The people who are lukewarm are going to have a very difficult time. People who are sitting on the fence are going to be moved. When the Spirit of the Lord comes in like a flood, you are going to get washed off the fence. The best thing to do would be to get off the fence now, become on fire for God, and get into the camp of the army of the Lord.

I began to change my attention. I became more diligent. I knew I had to change my heart if I wanted to be a part of the army. Jesus knocked at the door of my heart that night and I heard His voice and opened the door. That army is an overcoming army! I volunteered! I enlisted! I am so glad I did. I offered my body as a living sacrifice.

What did I do? I stirred myself up on purpose. That is what Daniel did. He stirred himself to lay hold of God. The Word says, *"Draw nigh to God, and he will draw nigh to you"* (James 4:8).

If you were on fire for God at one time, and you are not now, you will have to stir yourself up. Stir yourself up with spiritual things. Begin to pray. Pray in the spirit. Build yourself up on your most holy faith. Begin to study the Word like you have never studied it before. Believe and act on everything God says to you. You can do exactly what I did. You can purpose in your heart that you won't be lazy about spiritual things. If you are, you are not going to walk after the spirit and walk in victory. *"For they that are after the flesh do mind the things of the flesh; but they that are after the Spirit the things of the Spirit. For to be carnally minded is death; but to be spiritually minded is life and peace"* (Romans 8:5-6). To live in life and peace is the best there is!

Earlier we offered our bodies as living sacrifices. That means we are no longer going to live to please ourselves. We are going to live to please God.

Living After the Spirit

"For if ye live after the flesh, ye shall die: but if ye through the Spirit do mortify the deeds of the body, ye shall live. For as many as are led by the Spirit of God, they are the sons of God" (Romans 8:13-14).

We have studied about suffering. The same suffering Jesus endured when He was crucified, we are to bear in our own bodies. We are to crucify our flesh, to mortify the deeds of the body, to command our flesh to follow after the Lord, as we follow after the Lord.

We have the power to overcome sin in the flesh because of what Jesus did on the cross.

> **For God has done what the Law could not do, [its power] being weakened by the flesh [the entire nature of man without the Holy Spirit]. Sending His own Son in the guise of sinful flesh and as an offering for sin, [God] condemned sin in the flesh [subdued, overcame, deprived it of its power over all who accept that sacrifice].**
>
> **(Romans 8:3, AMP)**

"For I reckon that the sufferings of this present time are not worthy to be compared with the glory which shall be revealed in us" (Romans 8:18). This suffering we do—this crucifying of the flesh, this mortifying the deeds of the flesh—is connected in the Scriptures with the glory of God. Why? Because God cannot

manifest Himself in His people if they follow after the flesh instead of after the Spirit of God.

God works in the spirit realm. As we follow after the Spirit, He works in us. We must lay aside natural things in the natural life, and take up the things of the spiritual life. As we walk in the spirit, the glory of God that is in the face of Jesus Christ will begin to be reflected in us. Crucifying the flesh and the glory of God revealed in us are connected together, scripture after scripture!

"Because the creature itself also shall be delivered from the bondage of corruption into the glorious liberty of the children of God" (Romans 8:21). God is wanting us to come to a place where we walk and live in this earth in the glorious liberty that has been prepared for us from the foundation of the world.

God made man to live in His glory. He crowned Adam with glory and honor (Psalm 8:5). Adam had the glory of God on him. He looked just like God. He wore a garment of light and had the same power and authority and appearance as God Himself. He was in God's image—His exact likeness.

That is why he had no realization of being naked until after he had sinned. When he sinned against God, spiritual life departed and spiritual death came. The glory that was his covering disappeared. All of God's creatures except man have their own covering. Birds are covered with feathers that are produced from within. Animals are covered with fur that is produced from within.

Adam and Eve's bodies were covered with an enswathement of glory which was produced from within their beings *(Word Studies in the Greek New Testament, Volume III)*. The life of God in Adam radiated the glory of God through Adam's flesh.

Sin brings man short of the glory of God. When Adam disobeyed God, he lost the power from within to produce and bring forth this glory. He had no life in him to manifest this covering. Spiritual death entered into him and only darkness could emanate. There was no longer any glory in Adam to be revealed. What a devastating blow to God's man whom God created in His own image. God told Moses, *"As truly as I live, all the earth shall be filled with the glory of the Lord"* (Numbers 14:21).

That is still God's plan today—for His glory to fill the earth. And His glory is revealed in the Church of Jesus Christ. His glory is revealed in us.

God has glorious liberty for us. This liberty is in walking after the spirit and not after the flesh. It is in the spirit realm. You and I are spirit beings. We live in flesh bodies. We are strange and peculiar creatures. We are spirits in natural bodies. God is calling us to be dominated by His Spirit and to bring our bodies of flesh under His control.

The Church will come to a place where we will walk with God. We will be like Enoch. The Bible says, "Enoch walked with God and God took him" (paraphrase). And in Hebrews it says Enoch was translated by faith and that he had the testimony that he pleased God. One day Enoch just went so far in the spirit, he did not come back. The Bible says he did not see death.

Isn't that what is going to happen with the Church who is looking for His appearance? We are going to be caught up with Him in the air. We are not going to see death. Paul said, *"Behold I show you a mystery; We shall not all sleep, but we shall all be changed."*

I believe the day of His appearing is at hand. We read in Ephesians what the Church will look like when Jesus comes to receive us: *"That he might sanctify and cleanse it with the washing of water by the word, That he might present it to himself a glorious church, not having spot, or wrinkle, or any such thing; but that it should be holy and without blemish"* (Ephesians 5:26-27).

A glorious Church! A Church full of the glory of God! A Church with no spots or wrinkles, but a holy Church without blemish. God wants us to learn how to listen to His Spirit so He can lead us into all truth and teach us how to remove the spots and wrinkles. He wants to be able to reveal His glory in us.

The Russian believers (prior to the changes in Eastern Europe) had to rely on the Spirit more than we do now, because of adverse circumstances. The underground church met in secret. Someone who had been ministering in the underground church told me about one instance. They met out in the woods and in different places. (It had to be a secret or they would be raided.) There was a spy in the camp and everywhere they went the KGB would show up.

They decided, "Well, all right, if you're going to come to the meeting, you'll have to get the information from the Spirit of God." They would have to pray and listen to God to know where to meet. At the next meeting, they had every person in that group show up except one. They knew who the guilty party was.

Walking in the spirit is real. Listening to the Holy Spirit is a way of life we must develop in order to fulfill what we are called to do in these last days.

We have the ability to listen to our spirit the same way. But we receive a newsletter every month that tells us where to meet. We have not had to depend on the Spirit's direction the way our Russian brothers and sisters had to. Nevertheless, it is just as available to us! Many of them haven't had Bibles and have had to be led by their spirit.

The people in the New Testament did not have Bibles to read. They also had to be led by their spirit. Paul told them to pray in the spirit so they would get the mind of the Spirit. Those people in Russia had to have the mind of the Spirit or they could not go to church!

Thank God, we live in a free land. But we must learn to walk in obedience to the Spirit while we are in liberty. Not being forced into it, but rather choosing the things of the spirit over the things of the world.

God is raising a people called the "Glorious Church," who can hear the voice of His Spirit and obey Him in whatever we are told to do. How can you know what the mind of the Spirit is? By renewing your mind with the Word of God, by praying in the spirit and by being sensitive to Him and by yielding your life, thoughts and direction to Him.

If you don't pull aside and take time to listen to God, you are not going to know the direction of the Holy Spirit. You are going to miss the great things

God has for your life. The time for being cold is over. The time for being lukewarm is over. It is time to rise up and become on fire and stay that way!

Purpose in your heart that you will not be lazy, that you will not draw back, hold back or sit down. Purpose in your heart that you will rise up and march forward and become on fire.

Prayer for Salvation
and Baptism in the Holy Spirit

Heavenly Father, I come to You in the Name of Jesus. Your Word says, *"Whosoever shall call on the name of the Lord shall be saved"* (Acts 2:21). I am calling on You. I pray and ask Jesus to come into my heart and be Lord over my life according to Romans 10:9-10. *"If thou shalt confess with thy mouth the Lord Jesus, and shalt believe in thine heart that God hath raised him from the dead, thou shalt be saved. For with the heart man believeth unto righteousness; and with the mouth confession is made unto salvation."* I do that now. I confess that Jesus is Lord, and I believe in my heart that God raised Him from the dead.

I am now reborn! I am a Christian—a child of Almighty God! I am saved! You also said in Your Word, *"If ye then, being evil, know how to give good gifts unto your children: HOW MUCH MORE shall your heavenly Father give the Holy Spirit to them that ask him?"* (Luke 11:13). I'm also asking You to fill me with the Holy Spirit. Holy Spirit, rise up within me as I praise God. I fully expect to speak with other tongues as You give me the utterance (Acts 2:4).

Begin to praise God for filling you with the Holy Spirit. Speak those words and syllables you receive—not in your own language, but the language given to you by the Holy Spirit. You have to use your own voice. God will not force you to speak. Worship and praise Him in your heavenly language—in other tongues.

Continue with the blessing God has given you and pray in tongues each day.

You are a born-again, Spirit-filled believer. You'll never be the same!

Find a good Word of God preaching church, and become a part of a church family who will love and care for you as you love and care for them.

We need to be connected to each other. It increases our strength in God. It's God's plan for us.

About the Author

Gloria Copeland is an author and minister of the gospel whose teaching ministry is known throughout the world. Believers worldwide know her through Believers' Conventions, Victory Campaigns, magazine articles, teaching tapes and videos, and the daily and Sunday *Believer's Voice of Victory* television broadcast, which she hosts with her husband, Kenneth Copeland. She is known for "Healing School," which she began teaching and hosting in 1979 at KCM meetings. Gloria delivers the Word of God and the keys to victorious Christian living to millions of people every year.

Gloria has written many books, including *God's Will for You, Walk With God, God's Will Is Prosperity, Hidden Treasures* and *Are You Listening.* She has also co-authored several books with her husband, including *Family Promises, Healing Promises* and the best-selling daily devotional, *Pursuit of His Presence.*

She holds an honorary doctorate from Oral Roberts University. In 1994, Gloria was voted Christian Woman of the Year, an honor conferred on women whose example demonstrates outstanding Christian leadership. Gloria is also the co-founder and vice president of Kenneth Copeland Ministries in Fort Worth, Texas.

Learn more about Kenneth Copeland Ministries by visiting our Web site at **www.kcm.org**.

Materials to Help You
Receive Your Healing
by Gloria Copeland

Books
* And Jesus Healed Them All
    God's Prescription for Divine Health
    God's Will for Your Healing
* Harvest of Health

Audiotapes
    God Is a Good God
    God Wants You Well
    Healing School

Videotapes
    Healing School: God Wants You Well

Books Available From
Kenneth Copeland Ministries

by Gloria Copeland
* And Jesus Healed Them All
  Are You Listening?
  Are You Ready?
  Build Your Financial Foundation
  Build Yourself an Ark
  Fight On!
  God's Prescription for Divine Health
  God's Success Formula
  God's Will for You
  God's Will for Your Healing
  God's Will Is Prosperity
* God's Will Is the Holy Spirit
* Harvest of Health
  Hidden Treasures
  Living Contact
  Living in Heaven's Blessings Now
* Love—The Secret to Your Success
  No Deposit—No Return
  Pleasing the Father
  Pressing In—It's Worth It All
  Shine On!
  The Power to Live a New Life
  The Unbeatable Spirit of Faith
* Walk in the Spirit
  Walk With God
  Well Worth the Wait

by Kenneth Copeland
* A Ceremony of Marriage
  A Matter of Choice
  Covenant of Blood
  Faith and Patience—The Power Twins

* Freedom From Fear
 Giving and Receiving
 Honor—Walking in Honesty, Truth and Integrity
 How to Conquer Strife
 How to Discipline Your Flesh
 How to Receive Communion
 Living at the End of Time—A Time of Supernatural Increase
 Love Never Fails
 Managing God's Mutual Funds
* Now Are We in Christ Jesus
* Our Covenant With God
 Partnership, Sharing the Vision—Sharing the Grace
* Prayer—Your Foundation for Success
* Prosperity: The Choice Is Yours
 Rumors of War
* Sensitivity of Heart
* Six Steps to Excellence in Ministry
* Sorrow Not! Winning Over Grief and Sorrow
* The Decision Is Yours
* The Force of Faith
* The Force of Righteousness
 The Image of God in You
 The Laws of Prosperity
* The Mercy of God
 The Miraculous Realm of God's Love
 The Outpouring of the Spirit—The Result of Prayer
* The Power of the Tongue
 The Power to Be Forever Free
 The Troublemaker
* The Winning Attitude
 Turn Your Hurts Into Harvests
* Welcome to the Family
* You Are Healed!
 Your Right-Standing With God

Books Co-Authored by Kenneth and Gloria Copeland
 Family Promises
 Healing Promises

Prosperity Promises
Protection Promises

*   From Faith to Faith—A Daily Guide to Victory
From Faith to Faith—A Perpetual Calendar

One Word From God Series
- One Word From God Can Change Your Destiny
- One Word From God Can Change Your Family
- One Word From God Can Change Your Finances
- One Word From God Can Change Your Formula
  for Success
- One Word From God Can Change Your Health
- One Word From God Can Change Your Nation
- One Word From God Can Change Your Prayer Life
- One Word From God Can Change Your Relationships

Over The Edge—A Youth Devotional
Over the Edge Xtreme Planner for Students—
      Designed for the School Year

Pursuit of His Presence—A Daily Devotional
Pursuit of His Presence—A Perpetual Calendar

Other Books Published by KCP
The First 30 Years—A Journey of Faith
      The story of the lives of Kenneth and Gloria Copeland.
Real People. Real Needs. Real Victories.
      A book of testimonies to encourage your faith.

John G. Lake—His Life, His Sermons, His Boldness of Faith
The Holiest of All by Andrew Murray
The New Testament in Modern Speech by
      Richard Francis Weymouth

Products Designed for Today's Children and Youth
Baby Praise Board Book
Baby Praise Christmas Board Book
Noah's Ark Coloring Book

The Best of *Shout!* Adventure Comics
The *Shout!* Joke Book
The *Shout!* Super-Activity Book

*Commander Kellie and the Superkids*_{SM} **Books:**
The SWORD Adventure Book
*Commander Kellie and the Superkids*_{SM} Series
Middle Grade Novels by Christopher P.N. Maselli
#1 The Mysterious Presence
#2 The Quest for the Second Half
#3 Escape From Jungle Island
#4 In Pursuit of the Enemy

*Available in Spanish

World Offices
of Kenneth Copeland Ministries

For more information about KCM and a free
catalog, please write the office nearest you.

Kenneth Copeland Ministries
Fort Worth, Texas 76192-0001

Kenneth Copeland
Locked Bag 2600
Mansfield Delivery Centre
QUEENSLAND 4122
AUSTRALIA

Kenneth Copeland
Post Office Box 15
BATH
BA1 3XN
ENGLAND U.K.

Kenneth Copeland
Private Bag X 909
FONTAINEBLEAU
2032
REPUBLIC OF SOUTH AFRICA

Kenneth Copeland
Post Office Box 378
Surrey, British Columbia
V3T 5B6
CANADA

UKRAINE
L'VIV 290000
Post Office Box 84
Kenneth Copeland Ministries
L'VIV 290000
UKRAINE

We're Here for You!

Believer's Voice of Victory Television Broadcast

Join Kenneth and Gloria Copeland and the *Believer's Voice of Victory* broadcasts Monday through Friday and on Sunday each week, and learn how faith in God's Word can take your life from ordinary to extraordinary. This teaching from God's Word is designed to get you where you want to be—*on top!*

You can catch the *Believer's Voice of Victory* broadcast on your local, cable or satellite channels.

*Check your local listings for times and stations in your area.

Believer's Voice of Victory Magazine

Enjoy inspired teaching and encouragement from Kenneth and Gloria Copeland and guest ministers each month in the *Believer's Voice of Victory* magazine. Also included are real-life testimonies of God's miraculous power and divine intervention into the lives of people just like you!

It's more than just a magazine—it's a ministry.

Shout! ...The dynamic magazine just for kids!

Shout! The Voice of Victory for Kids is a Bible-charged, action-packed, bimonthly magazine available FREE to kids everywhere! Featuring *Wichita Slim* and *Commander Kellie and the Superkids, Shout!* is filled with colorful adventure comics, challenging games and puzzles, exciting short stories, solve-it-yourself mysteries and much more!!

Stand up, sign up and get ready to *Shout!*

To receive a FREE subscription to *Believer's Voice of Victory,* or to give a child you know a FREE subscription to *Shout!,* write:

Kenneth Copeland Ministries
Fort Worth, Texas 76192-0001

Or call:
1-800-600-7395
(9 a.m.-5 p.m. CT)

Or visit our Web site at:
www.kcm.org

If you are writing from outside the U.S., please contact the KCM office nearest you. Addresses for all Kenneth Copeland Ministries offices are listed on the previous page.

The Harrison House Vision

Proclaiming the truth and the power

Of the Gospel of Jesus Christ

With excellence;

Challenging Christians to

Live victoriously,

Grow spiritually,

Know God intimately.

If this book has changed your life, we would like to hear from you. Please write us at:

Harrison House Publishers

P.O. Box 35035 • Tulsa, Oklahoma 74153

You can also visit us on the web at

www.harrisonhouse.com